Professor Hoffmann's
Best Math and Logic Puzzles

Louis Hoffmann

Dover Publications, Inc.
Mineola, New York

CONTENTS

Bibliographical Note

This Dover edition, first published in 2007, contains a new selection of puzzles from *Puzzles Old and New,* originally published by Frederick Warne and Co., London and New York, in 1893.

Library of Congress Cataloging-in-Publication Data

Hoffmann, Professor, 1839–1919.
    [Best math and logic puzzles]
    Professor Hoffmann's best math and logic puzzles / Louis Hoffmann. — Dover ed.
      p. cm.
    Originally published: Puzzles, old, and new. London : F. Warne, c1893.
    ISBN 0-486-45474-6 (pbk.)
    1. Mathematical recreations. 2. Logic puzzles. I. Title. II. Title: Best math and logic puzzles.

QA95.H63 2007
793.74—dc22

2006102939

Manufactured in the United States of America
Dover Publications, Inc., 31 East 2nd Street, Mineola, N.Y. 11501

CHAPTER I.

No. I.—The "Forty-five" Puzzle.

THE number 45 has some curious properties. Among others, it may be divided into four parts, in such manner that if you add two to the first, subtract two from the second, multiply the third by two, and divide the fourth by two, the result will in each case be equal.

What are they ?

No. II.—A Singular Subtraction.

Required, to subtract 45 from 45 in such manner that there shall be 45 left.

No. III.—A Mysterious Multiplicand.

Required, to find a number which, multiplied by 3, 6, 9, 12, 15, 18, 21, 24, or 27, shall in each case give as product the same digit, three times repeated.

No. IV.—Counting the Pigs.

A youngster asked a farmer how many pigs he had. "You shall reckon for yourself," said the farmer. "If I had as many more, and half as many more, and seven to boot, I should have 32."

How many had he?

1

No. V.—Another "Pig" Problem.

A farmer, being asked the same question, replied, "If I had as many more, and half as many more, and two pigs and a half, I should have just a score."

How many had he?

No. VI.—A Little Miscalculation.

A market-woman bought 120 apples at four a penny, and the same number of another sort at six a penny; but finding that they were beginning to spoil, determined to sell them off at cost-price. To save trouble, she mixed them together and sold them at ten for twopence, expecting to just get her money back again. But when all were sold, she found, to her surprise, that she had lost twopence over the transaction.

How did this happen?

No. VII.—A Simple Magic Square.

Required, to arrange the numbers 1 to 9 inclusive in the form of a square, in such manner that the total of each line, whether horizontal, vertical, or diagonal, shall be the same—viz., 15.

No. VIII.—The "Thirty-four" Puzzle.

Required, to arrange the numbers 1 to 16 inclusive in the form of a square, in such manner that the total of each line, horizontal, vertical, or diagonal, shall be the same—viz., 34.

No. IX.—The "Sixty-five" Puzzle.

Required, to arrange the numbers 1 to 25 inclusive in the form of a square, under the same conditions, the total being 65 each way.

No. X.—The "Twenty-six" Puzzle.

This is a magic square with a difference, the four corner places being omitted. The problem is to arrange the numbers 1 to 12 inclusive in the form of a cross, as shown in Fig. 334, so as to make 26 in seven different ways—viz., the two horizontal and the two vertical rows, the group of squares marked *a a a a*, the group marked *b b b b*, and

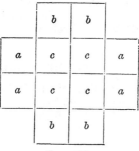

FIG. 334.

the group marked *c c c c*, each making the above-mentioned total.

No. XI.—An Unmanageable Legacy.

An old farmer left a will whereby he bequeathed his horses to his three sons, John, James, and William, in the following proportions : John, the eldest, was to have one half, James to have one-third, and William one-ninth. When he died, however, it was found that the number of horses in his stable was seventeen, a number which is divisible neither by two, by three, or by nine. In their perplexity the three brothers consulted a clever lawyer, who hit on a scheme whereby the intentions of the testator were carried out to the satisfaction of all parties.

How was it managed ?

No. XII.—Many Figures, but a Small Result.

Required, of the numbers 1, 2, 3, 4, 5, 6, 7, 8, 9, 0, to compose two fractions, whose sum shall be equal to unity. Each number to be used once, and once only.

No. XIII.—Can You Name It ?

Required, to find a number which is just so much short of 50 as its quadruple is above 50.

No. XIV.—Squares, Product, and Difference.

Required, to find two numbers the sum of whose squares is greater by 181 than their product, and whose product is greater by 161 than their difference.

No. XV.—A Peculiar Number.

Required, to find a number of six digits of such a nature that if you transfer the two left-hand digits (28) to the opposite end, the new number thus formed is exactly double the original number.

No. XVI.—A Novel Century.

Required, by multiplication and addition of the numbers 1 to 9 inclusive, to make 100, each number being used once, and once only.

No. XVII.—Another Century.

Required, by addition only of the numbers 1 to 9 inclusive to make 100, each number being used once, and once only.

No. XVIII.—Another Way to make a Hundred.

Required, with six nines to express the number 100.

No. XIX.—The Lucky Number.

Many persons have what they consider a " lucky " number. Show such a person the row of figures subjoined—

1, 2, 3, 4, 5, 6, 7, 9,

(consisting of the numerals from 1 to 9 inclusive, with the 8 only omitted), and inquire what is his lucky or favourite number. He names any number he pleases from 1 to 9, say 7. You reply that, as he is fond of sevens, he shall have plenty of them, and accordingly proceed to multiply the series above given by such a number that the resulting product consists of sevens only.

Required, to find (for each number that may be selected) the multiplier which will produce the above result.

No. XX.—The Two Ages.

Father and son are aged 71 and 34 respectively. At what age was the father three times the age of his son; and at what age will the latter have reached half his father's age?

No. XXI.—The Graces and the Muses.

The three Graces, each bearing a like number of roses, one day met the nine Muses. Each Grace gave to each Muse the eighteenth part of her store, when it was found that each Muse had twelve roses less than each of the three Graces.

What number of roses had each Grace originally?

No. XXII.—The Graces and the Muses Again.

Sometimes the puzzle is stated in another form. The three Graces, laden with roses as before, meet the nine Muses, and each Grace gives to each Muse such a proportion of her store that when the division is complete, each Grace and each Muse has an equal share.

How many roses had each Grace at first?

No. XXIII.—Just One Over.

A man, being asked how many sovereigns he had in his pocket, replied, "If I divide them by 2, by 3, by 4, by 5, or by 6, I shall always have one over."

What number had he?

No. XXIV.—Scarcely Explicit.

Another person, being asked a similar question, replied, "If I had half as much more, two-thirds as much more, three-fourths as much more, four-fifths as much more, five-sixths as much more, and nine sovereigns to boot, I should have exactly £100."

How much had he?

No. XXV.—Making Things Even.

Two children were discussing their pocket-money. "If you were to give me a penny," said Johnny, "I should have twice as much as you." "That would not be a fair division," said Tommy; "you had better give me a penny, and then we shall be just alike."

How much money had each?

No. XXVI.—A Rejected Proposal.

A little later Johnny and Tommy met again. "I have now just twice as much as you have," said Johnny; "but if you were to give me a penny I should have three times as much." "No, thank you," said Tommy; "but give me two-pence, and we shall be equal."

How much had each?

No. XXVII.—The Market-woman and her Stock.

A woman selling apples met three boys. The first bought half her stock, and gave her back 10; the second bought a third of what she had then remaining, and gave her back 2; and the third bought half of her then remaining store, and gave her back 1; after which she found that she had 12 apples left.

How many had she at first?

No. XXVIII.—The Captives in the Tower.

An elderly queen, her daughter, and little son, weighing 195 pounds, 105 pounds, and 90 pounds respectively, were kept prisoners at the top of a high tower. The only communication with the ground below was a cord passing over a pulley, with a basket at each end, and so arranged that when one basket rested on the ground the other was opposite the window. Naturally, if the one were more heavily loaded than the other, the heavier would descend; but if the excess on either side was more than 15 pounds, the descent became so rapid as to be dangerous, and from the position of the rope the captives could not check it with their hands. The only thing available to help them in the tower was a cannon-ball, weighing 75 pounds. They, notwithstanding, contrived to escape.

How did they manage it?

No. XXIX.—Father and Son.

A father aged 45 has a son of 12.
How soon will the father be only three times the age of the son ?

No. XXX.—A Complicated Transaction.

William gives Thomas as many shillings as Thomas has. Thomas then gives William as many shillings as William has left. This done, William has 36 shillings, and Thomas 42 shillings.
How much had each at first ?

No. XXXI.—A Long Family.

A farmer and his wife have fifteen children, born at regular intervals, there being a difference in each case of a year and a half. The eldest is eight times the age of the youngest.
How old must the latter be ?

No. XXXII.—A Curious Number.

A certain number is divisible into four parts; in such manner that the first is 500 times, the second 400 times, and the third 40 times as much as the last and smallest part.
What is the number, and what are the several parts ?

No. XXXIII.—The Shepherd and his Sheep.

A shepherd was asked how many sheep he had in his flock. He replied that he could not say, but he knew if he counted them by twos, by threes, by fours, by fives, or by sixes, there was always one over; but if he counted them by sevens, there was none over.
What is the smallest number which will answer the above conditions ?

No. XXXIV.—A Difficult Problem.

What is the smallest number which, divided by 2, will give a remainder of 1 ; divided by 3, a remainder of 2 ; divided by 4, a remainder of 3 ; divided by 5, a remainder of

4; divided by 6, a remainder of 5; divided by 7, a remainder of 6; divided by 8, a remainder of 7; divided by 9, a remainder of 8; and divided by 10, a remainder of 9.

No. XXXV.—Well Laid Out.

A lad went into a shop to buy drawing materials. He found that pencils cost twopence each, sheets of paper threepence, and drawing-pins a halfpenny, while indiarubber was fourpence. He bought a supply of each, spending two shillings, and found that he had exactly twenty-one articles.

What were they?

No. XXXVI.—The Two Travellers.

A and *B* are travelling the same road, *A* going four miles an hour, *B* five miles an hour. But *A* has two and a half hours' start.

In what length of time will *B* overtake *A*, and how far from the starting-point?

No. XXXVII.—Measuring the Garden.

A garden, oblong in shape, is three times as long as it is wide. If it were a yard more each way, its area would be increased by 149 square yards.

What are its dimensions?

No. XXXVIII.—When Will They get It?

Seven guests at a restaurant came, the first every day, the second every other day, the third every third day, and so on to the seventh, who came once a week only. The host, in a liberal mood, declared that on the first day all came together he would treat them to a dinner gratis.

How soon, according to the above order of rotation, would they be in a position to claim his promise?

No. XXXIX.—Passing the Gate.

It was the rule in a certain continental town that any one passing through either of the four city gates, whether going out or coming in, should pay a penny. A stranger arrived one day at the town, paid his penny and passed through the first gate. He spent in the town one half of the money he had left, and then went out again by the same gate, again paying a penny. The next day he did the like, entering and passing out by the second gate, and meanwhile spending half his available cash in the town. On the following two days he did the same, entering and leaving by the third and fourth gates respectively. When he left the town for the fourth time he had only one penny left.

How much had he at first?

No. XL.—A Novel Magic Square.

Required, to arrange the numbers 1 to 81 in the form of a magic square, in such manner that after removing the outermost rows you still have a magic square, and so on, removing row by row with the same result until only the number occupying the central square remains, which number shall be the greatest common divisor of the sums of the several squares.

No. XLI.—Another Magic Square.

Required, to form with the series of numbers 0, 1, 2, etc., to 63 inclusive, a magic square of 64 places, in such manner that the total of each horizontal or vertical line shall be 252; if the principal square be broken up into four smaller ones of sixteen places each, the total of each horizontal or vertical line shall be 126; and if each of these smaller squares be again broken up into four squares of four places each, the total of the numbers in each such four places shall again be 126.

No. XLII.—The Set of Weights.

With what five weights can a man weigh any quantity (proceeding by steps of half a pound) from half a pound up to 60 lbs.?

No. XLIII.—What Did He Lose?

A man goes into a shop and buys a hat, price one guinea. He offers in payment for it a £5 note. The hatter gets the note cashed by a neighbour, the purchaser pocketing his change, £3 19s., and walking off with the hat. No sooner has he left, however, than the neighbour who changed the note comes in with the news that it is a counterfeit, and the hatter has to refund the value.

How much is the hatter out of pocket by the transaction?

No. XLIV.—A Difficult Division.

A wine merchant has in his cellar 21 casks. Seven are full of wine; seven half-full, and seven empty.

How can he divide them (without transferring any portion of the liquid from cask to cask) among his three sons —Dick, Tom, and Harry—so that each shall have not only an equal quantity of wine, but an equal number of casks?

No. XLV.—The Hundred Bottles of Wine.

An innkeeper sold in eight days 100 bottles of wine, each day overpassing by three bottles the quantity sold on the previous day.

How many did he sell on the first, and on each of the succeeding days?

No. XLVI.—The Last of Her Stock.

An old market woman, finding that she had but a few apples left, divided them among her three grandchildren, as follows: to Willie she gave half her stock and one apple over; to Tommy half what she had then left and one apple over; and to Jennie half what she had still left and one apple over. This done, she had none left.

How many apples did she divide?

No. XLVII.—The Walking Match.

Three persons, *A, B, C, D*, start from the same point to walk round a circular piece of ground, whose circumference is one mile. *A* walks five miles an hour, *B* four miles, *C* three miles, and *D* two miles an hour.

How long will it be before all four again meet at the starting-point?

No. XLVIII.—A Feat of Divination.

A couple of dice are thrown. The thrower is invited to double the points of one of the dice (whichever he pleases), add 5 to the result, multiply by 5, and add the points of the second die. He states the total, when any one knowing the secret can instantly name the points of the two dice.

How is it done?

No. XLIX.—A Peculiar Number.

Required, a number of six digits, of such nature that if you transfer the first figure on the right hand (7) to the opposite end of the row, the number as thus altered will be five times the original number; or if you transfer the first figure on the left hand (1) to the opposite end, the resulting number shall be three times the original number. If again you transfer the three first (or three last) figures to the opposite end, the result will represent six times the original number.

No. L.—Another Peculiar Number.

What is the lowest number which, divided by 2, 3, 4, 5, or 6, leaves a remainder of 1, but divided by 11 leaves no remainder?

No. LI.—The Three Legacies.

A gentleman, making his will, left legacies to his three servants, of whom the parlourmaid had been with him three times as long as the housemaid, and the cook twice as long as the parlourmaid. He distributed his gifts in the same proportions; and the total amount given was £70.

What was the amount received by each?

No. LII.—Another Mysterious Multiplicand.

What number of two figures is that which, being multiplied by 3, 6, and 9 respectively, the three products together include every digit from 1 to 9 inclusive, each being only once employed?

No. LIII.—How to Divide Twelve among Thirteen.

A gentleman has a sum of twelve sovereigns to be distributed in charity, a sovereign to each approved candidate.
On the day of distribution thirteen claimants appear.   The
donor has reason to believe that one of them is a less de-
serving object than the rest, and desires to leave him out,
but without showing any apparent favouritism.   He directs
the claimants to stand in a circle, and announces that every
ninth man, as he counts round and round, shall step out of
the circle and receive his gift till the fund is exhausted, the
last man receiving nothing.

Where must the distributor begin to count, in order to
exclude the candidate he desires to reject ?

No. LIV.—Tenth Man Out.

A somewhat more difficult puzzle of the same class runs
as follows : The crew of a certain ship consisted of fifteen
white men and fifteen negroes.   A storm arising, it became
necessary to take to the boats, but these only afforded room
for half the number.   It was agreed that all should stand
in a circle, and that the captain should count round and
round the circle by tens, each tenth man to take his place
in the boat till the number of fifteen was reached, the
others to take their chance with the ship.

The captain, desiring to favour his own countrymen, so
placed the men that the fifteen blacks were all left behind.

How must the circle be arranged to effect this result ?

No. LV.—Ninth Man Out.

Given the same conditions, save that every *ninth* man,
instead of every tenth, is to go in the boat.

What will then be the arrangement of the circle ?

[Puzzles of the kind next immediately following have been
popular from very early times, one of the earliest known

collections, that of Bachet de Mezeriac, *Recueil de Problèmes plaisants et délectables qui se font par les nombres*, bearing date as far back as 1613. Though not exactly arithmetical, in the ordinary sense, they depend upon arithmetical principles, and are therefore inserted in this chapter.]

No. LVI.—The Three Travellers.

Three travellers, accompanied by their servants, arrive at the bank of a river and desire to cross. The only means of transit is a boat which carries two persons. The travellers have reason to believe that the servants have entered into a conspiracy to rob and murder them, should they be able to get the upper hand. It is therefore essential that a single master should not be left alone with two of the servants, or two masters with all three of the servants.

How can the transit be arranged so as to avoid either of the above conditions?

No. LVII.—The Wolf, the Goat, and the Cabbages.

A boatman has to ferry across a stream a wolf, a goat, and a basket of cabbages. His boat is so small that only one of the three, besides himself, can be contained in it. How is he to manage, so that the wolf shall have no opportunity of killing the goat, or the goat of eating up the cabbages?

No. LVIII.—The Three Jealous Husbands.

Three jealous husbands, travelling with their wives, find it necessary to cross a stream in a boat which only holds two persons. Each of the husbands has a great objection to his wife crossing with either of the other male members of the party unless he himself is also present.

How is the passage to be arranged?

No. LIX.—The Captain and His Company.

The captain of a company of soldiers, in the course of his day's march, comes to a river which must be crossed. The

only means of transit is a boat wherein two children are
paddling about, and which is so small that it will only hold
the two children or one grown person.

How is the transit to be effected?

No. LX.—The Treasure Trove.

An Irishman and a Scotchman, digging together in a field,
came upon a number of gold coins. When they were about
to divide them, the Scotchman, who was of an avaricious
turn, conceived a plan to outwit the Irishman and secure
the whole for himself. He therefore proposed to the Irishman that if, without asking any question, he could name
the exact number of coins he should take the whole; if he
failed, the other should take all. The Irishman readily
agreed, and counted the money, taking special care that
the Scotchman should not see how much it was. "Now
add 666 to it," said the Scotchman. "Done," replied the
Irishman. "Now, ye'll maybe subtract the whole amount
from 999." "Done again," replied the Irishman; "but the
divil a bit are ye nearer!" "Bide a wee," said the Scotchman. "Now jist pit down 333, and tak' awa the last
figures from it, and ye'll no be far off the tottle of the bit
money." "Mother o' Moses!" exclaimed the Irishman,
"somebody must have tould ye;" and the Scotchman walked
off with the treasure trove accordingly.

How did the Scotchman get at the right total?

No. LXI.—The Row of Counters.

This is in principle very similar to the last puzzle. In
point of fact it is the same thing, though in a different
form, and we therefore insert it next in order.

A spectator is invited to place upon the table two rows
of counters, unequal in number. The actual numbers are
immaterial, but may range, say, from ten to twenty. The
person who performs the trick is, meanwhile, blindfolded,
so that he can have no knowledge what the numbers are.
The person who has laid out the counters is then requested—

1. To subtract the smaller number from the larger, and
state the difference. (We will suppose that he states such
difference to be 3.)

2. To remove a certain number (say 5) from the smaller row.

3. To subtract the number remaining in the smaller row from the larger row. The number subtracted is to be removed altogether, as also what now remain of the smaller row.

4. The operator, without asking any further question, at once names the number left in the larger row.

How does he ascertain it?

No. LXII.—A Loan and a Present.

This is another puzzle on the same principle. It is usually presented in the shape of a conjuring trick. The operator requests some one to think of a given number of shillings, large or small, as he pleases. He is then in imagination to borrow the same amount from some member of the company, and add it to the original number. " Now please suppose," says the operator, " that I make you a present of fourteen shillings, and add that also. Now give half the total amount to the poor; then return the borrowed money, and tell the company how much you have remaining. I know already what it is; in fact, I hold in my hand the precise amount." " Seven," is the reply. The operator opens his hand and shows that it contains exactly seven shillings.

How is the amount ascertained?

No. LXIII.—Eleven Guests in Ten Beds.

An innkeeper had a sudden influx of guests, eleven arriving in one party, and demanding beds. The host had only ten beds at his disposal, but he, notwithstanding, managed to accommodate them as follows: he put two in the first bed, with the understanding that the second should have a bed to himself after a brief interval; he then put the third in the second bed, the fourth in the third bed, and so on, the tenth being accommodated in the ninth bed. He had thus one bed still left, which the eleventh man, now sleeping double in the first bed, was invited to occupy.

It is clear that there must be a fallacy somewhere, but where does it lie?

No. LXIV.—A Difficult Division.

A and *B* have purchased an eight-gallon cask of wine, and desire to divide it equally; but they have only two measures wherewith to do so—one a five-gallon and the other a three-gallon.

How are they to manage?

No. LXV.—The Three Market-Women.

Three peasant-women went to market to sell apples. The first had 33, the second 29, and the third 27 only. Each of them gave the same number of apples for a penny, and yet, when they got home, they found that each had received an equal amount of money.

How could such a result come to pass?

No. LXVI.—The Farmer and His Three Daughters.

This is a puzzle of the same kind, differing only in the figures.

A farmer sent his three daughters to the market to sell apples. The elder had 50, the second daughter 30, and the younger 10. The farmer jokingly told them all to sell at the same price, and bring home the same amount of money, and, to his surprise, they actually did so.

How did they manage it?

No. LXVII.—How Many for a Penny?

A boy purchased a pennyworth of apples. He gave to a playmate one-third of his store, and one-third of an apple over, after which he had exactly one apple left.

How many did he get for his penny?

No. LXVIII.—The Magic Cards.

These are usually presented as a conjuring trick, but they also form a very effective puzzle, for it is clear that the secret must lie in the cards themselves, and, given sufficient acuteness, must be discoverable.

Prepare seven cards with numbers on them as follows:—

I.	II.	III.	IV.
1 33 65 97	2 34 66 98	4 36 68 100	8 40 72 104
3 35 67 99	3 35 67 99	5 37 69 101	9 41 73 105
5 37 69 101	6 38 70 102	6 38 70 102	10 42 74 106
7 39 71 103	7 39 71 103	7 39 71 103	11 43 75 107
9 41 73 105	10 42 74 106	12 44 76 108	12 44 76 108
11 43 75 107	11 43 75 107	13 45 77 109	13 45 77 109
13 45 77 109	14 46 78 110	14 46 78 110	13 46 78 110
15 47 79 111	15 47 79 111	15 47 79 111	15 47 79 111
17 49 81 113	18 50 82 114	20 52 84 116	24 56 88 120
19 51 83 115	19 51 83 115	21 53 85 117	25 57 89 121
21 53 85 117	22 54 86 118	22 54 86 118	26 58 90 122
23 55 87 119	23 55 87 119	23 55 87 119	27 59 91 123
25 57 89 121	26 58 90 122	28 60 92 124	28 60 92 124
27 59 91 123	27 59 91 123	29 61 93 125	29 61 93 125
29 61 93 125	30 62 94 126	30 62 94 126	30 62 94 126
31 63 95 127	31 63 95 127	31 63 95 127	31 63 95 127

V.	VI.	VII.
16 48 80 112	32 48 96 112	64 80 96 112
17 49 81 113	33 49 97 113	65 81 97 113
18 50 82 114	34 50 98 114	66 82 98 114
19 51 83 115	35 51 99 115	67 83 99 115
20 52 84 116	36 52 100 116	68 84 100 116
21 53 85 117	37 53 101 117	69 85 101 117
22 54 86 118	38 54 102 118	70 86 102 118
23 55 87 119	39 55 103 119	71 87 103 119
24 56 88 120	40 56 104 120	72 88 104 120
25 57 89 121	41 57 105 121	73 89 105 121
26 58 90 122	42 58 106 122	74 90 106 122
27 59 91 123	43 59 107 123	75 91 107 123
28 60 92 124	44 60 108 124	76 92 108 124
29 61 93 125	45 61 109 125	77 93 109 125
30 62 94 126	46 62 110 126	78 94 110 126
31 63 95 127	47 63 111 127	79 95 111 127

A person is requested to think of any number, from 1 to 127 inclusive, and to state on which one or more of the seven cards it is to be found. Any one knowing the secret can instantly name the chosen number.

How is the number ascertained ?

No. LXIX.—The " Fifteen " or " Boss " Puzzle.

This, like a good many of the best puzzles, hails from America, where, some years ago, it had an extraordinary vogue, which a little later spread to this country, the

British public growing nearly as excited over the mystic "Fifteen" as they did at a later date over the less innocent "Missing Word" competitions.

The "Fifteen" Puzzle consists of a little flat wooden or cardboard box, wherein are arranged, in four rows, fifteen little cubical blocks, each bearing a number, from 1 to 15 inclusive. The box being square, would naturally accommodate 16 such cubes,* and there is therefore one space always vacant, and by means of such vacant space, the cubes may be shifted about in the box so as to assume different relative positions.

1	2	3	4
5	6	7	8
9	10	11	12
13	15	14	

Fig. 335.

The ordinary "Fifteen" Puzzle is, having placed the cubes in the box haphazard, so to move them about (without lifting, but merely pushing one after another into the space for the time being vacant) as to bring them into regular order from 1 to 15, leaving the vacant space at the right-hand bottom corner.

In what is known as the "Boss" or Master Puzzle all the blocks are in the first instance placed in regular order, with the exception of those numbered 14 and 15, which are reversed, as in Fig. 335.

---

* As a matter of fact, 16 cubes are usually supplied, the set thereby being made available for the "Thirty-four" Puzzle (referred to at p. 146). When the "Fifteen" Puzzle is attempted, the cube bearing the number 16 is removed from the box.

No. LXX.—The Peg-away Puzzle.

The "Peg-away" Puzzle (Perry & Co.) is a variation or modification of the "Fifteen" Puzzle, the difference being that there are nine instead of sixteen cells, and that eight instead

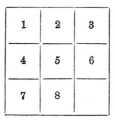

1	2	3
4	5	6
7	8	

FIG. 336.

of fifteen numbered blocks or "pegs" are used. These being arranged hap-hazard in the cells, the problem is to bring them into consecutive order, as shown in Fig. 336.

No. LXXI.—The Over-Polite Guests.

Seven gentlemen met to dine at a restaurant, when a question arose as to precedence, no one desiring to take what were regarded as the more honourable seats. To settle the matter, one of them proposed that they should dine together every day until they had respectively occupied all possible positions at the table; and the suggestion was accepted.

How often must they dine together to answer the above conditions ? *

---

* This problem is sometimes propounded in another shape, as follows : A party of seven students, with more wit than money, agreed with a restaurant-keeper to pay him £10 per head so soon as they should have occupied all possible positions at the table, he undertaking to entertain them daily in the meantime with a dinner costing half a crown per head.

Query, how much the host made or lost by the transaction?

No. LXXII.—The " Royal Aquarium " Thirteen Puzzle.*

This is an adaptation of the "Magic Square " idea, but modified in a very ingenious manner, the ordinary processes for forming a magic square being here quite inapplicable.

The puzzle consists of nine cards, not quite $1\frac{1}{2}$ inch each way, each bearing four numbers, radiating from the centre, after the manner shown in Fig. 337.

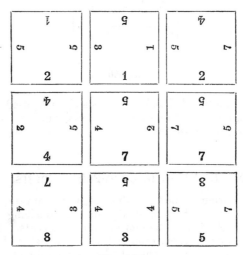

FIG. 337.

The figures shown in heavy type in the diagram are in the original printed in *red*.

The experimenter is required to arrange the nine cards in a square, the red numbers forming perpendicular lines, and the black numbers horizontal lines, the three figures in each line, whether horizontal or perpendicular, making, when added together, 13.

---

* Procurable at the Royal Aquarium, Westminster. Price 1*d*., or by post, with solution, 3*d*.

No. LXXIII.—An Easy Creditor.

A gentleman being in temporary need of money, a friend lent him £60, telling him to repay it in such sums as might suit his convenience. Shortly afterwards he made a payment on account. His second payment was half as much as the first; his third three-quarters as much; his fourth one-quarter as much, and his fifth two-fifths as much. It was then found, on striking a balance, that he still owed £2.

What was the amount of the first payment ?

No. LXXIV.—The Three Arabs.

Two Bedouin Arabs halted in the desert to eat their midday meal Their store consisted of eight small loaves, of which five belonged to the first, and three to the second. Just as they sat down, a third Arab overtook them, and asked to be permitted to share their meal, to which they agreed. Each ate an equal portion of the eight loaves, and the third Arab, at the close of the meal, handed the others eight pieces of money in payment. A dispute arose as to the division of the money, the first Arab maintaining that as he had had five loaves and the other three only, the money should be divided in the same proportion. The other maintained that as all had eaten equally, each should take half the money between them. Finally they agreed to refer the matter to the third Arab, who declared that both were in the wrong, and pointed out the proper division.

What was it ?

No. LXXV.—An Eccentric Testator.

An eccentric old gentleman left a will, whereby he bequeathed to his eldest son £110, and one-ninth of what remained ; to his second son £220, and one-ninth of what then remained ; to his third son £330, and one-ninth of the remainder ; and so on, each junior in turn taking £110 more by way of original gift, and one-ninth of the portion still remaining.

The legatees at first complained of so unequal a disposition, but on ascertaining the value of the estate and proceeding to a division, they found, to their surprise, that the division exactly exhausted the estate, and that the share of each was of exactly the same value.

How many legatees were there, and what was the total value of the estate ?

No. LXXVI.—Another Eccentric Testator.

A testator, having five sons, left his property as follows : To the eldest one-sixth of the whole, and £240 in addition. To the second one-fifth of the residue, and £288. To the third one-fourth of the then residue, and £360 To the fourth one-third of the then residue and £480. And to the fifth one-half of what still remained, and £720. There was then nothing left.

What was the amount of the property, and what was the share of each son ?

No. LXXVII.—An Aggravating Uncle.

An uncle with a turn for figures presented his youthful nephew with a box of soldiers, but made it a condition that he should not play with them till he could discover, on arithmetical principles, how many the box contained. He was told that if he placed them three in a row, there would be one over; if he placed them four in a row, there would be two over; if five in a row, three over; if six in a row, he would have four over. The total number was under 100.

How many soldiers did the box contain ?

No. LXXVIII.—Apples and Oranges.

A paterfamilias brought home a quantity of apples and oranges, the same number of each, and distributed them among his children. After each child had received 12 apples there were 48 over, and after each child had received 15 oranges there were 15 over.

How many were there of each kind of fruit, and among how many children were they divided ?

No. LXXIX.—The Two Squares.

A certain number of counters, if arranged in rows so as to form a square, leave a remainder of 146 counters unemployed. To enlarge the square by an additional row each way 31 more counters would be required.

What is the number of counters ?

No. LXXX.—A Curious Division.

Required, to divide 7890 counters into three heaps, in such proportions that if the first heap be divided by three, the second by six, and the third by nine, the quotient shall in each case be the same number.

No. LXXXI.—A Curious Multiplication.

Required, to divide the same number (7890) of counters into four heaps, in such proportions that if the first be multiplied by three, the second by four, the third by six, and the fourth by twelve, the product shall in each case be the same.

No. LXXXII.—The Two Schoolmasters.

Two country schoolmasters were discussing their respective schools. The first said, "One-sixth of my pupils are away ill, eleven are haymaking, seven are gone to the fair, and I have thirty-seven here at work." The other replied, "You have a pretty large school, but mine is larger than yours, for I have seventy-two pupils."

What was the difference of their numbers ?

No. LXXXIII.—Nothing Left.

There is a certain number from which, if you subtract ten, multiply the remainder by three, find the square root of the product, and from such square root subtract eighteen, nothing is left.

What is the number ?

No. LXXXIV.—The Three Generations.

An old man was asked how old he was. He replied, "The united ages of my son and myself are 109 years; those of my son and my grandson are 56 years; and my grandson and myself together number 85 years."

How old was each ?

No. LXXXV.—The Two Brothers.

"How old is your brother?" a man was asked. "Two-thirds of his age," he replied, "is just five-twelfths of mine, and I am nine years older than he."
What was the age of each?

No. LXXXVI.—The Two Sons.

An elderly mathematician was asked what were the ages of his two sons. He replied, "The one is five and a quarter years older than the other, and six times the age of the elder, added to five times the age of the younger, would be 301."
What was the age of each?

No. LXXXVII.—The Two Nephews.

The same man was asked the ages of his two nephews. "The elder," he replied, "is just three times as old as the younger, and if you add together the squares of their ages, the total will be 360."
What was the age of each?

No. LXXXVIII.—The Reversed Number.

There is a number consisting of two digits; the number itself is equal to five times the sum of its digits, and if nine be added to the number, the position of its digits is reversed.
What is the number?

No. LXXXIX.—Another Reversed Number.

There is another number of two digits, which itself is equal to seven times the sum of its digits. If 18 be subtracted from it, the position of its digits is reversed.
What is the number?

No. XC.—The Shepherd and his Sheep.

A shepherd was asked how many sheep he had. He replied, "I have 100, in five sheep-folds. In the first and second there are altogether 52 sheep; in the second and third, 43; in the third and fourth, 34; and in the fourth and fifth, 30."
How many sheep had he in each fold?

No. XCI.—The Shepherdess and her Sheep.

A shepherdess had the care of a number of sheep, in four different folds. In the second were twice as many as the first, in the third twice as many as the second, and in the fourth twice as many as the third. The total number was 105.

How many sheep were there in each fold ?

No. XCII.—A Weighty Matter.

With how many weights, and of what denominations respectively, can you weigh any number of pounds from 1 to 127 inclusive?

No. XCIII.—The Three Topers.

Three topers were discussing how long it would take each of them to drink forty quarts of lager beer. Peter undertook to do it between four in the morning and twelve at night; Paul between ten in the morning and twelve at night; and Roger between two in the afternoon and twelve at night.

Assuming that they could do as they boasted, how long would it take them to get through the same quantity, all drinking simultaneously ?

No. XCIV.—The False Scales.

A cheese put into one of the scales of a false balance was found to weigh 16 lbs. When placed in the opposite scale it weighed 9 lbs. only.

What was its actual weight ?

No. XCV.—An Arithmetical Policeman.

A belated reveller, hearing the clock strike, but being too obfuscated to be quite sure as to the number of strokes, proceeded to "ask a policeman" what time it was. The policeman replied, "Take half, a third, and a fourth of the hour that has just struck, and the total will be one larger."

What was the hour ?

No. XCVI.—The Flock of Geese.

Two friends, passing a woman with a flock of geese, made a wager as to who should guess nearest at their number, without actually counting, one maintaining that there were not more than thirty, the other that there were over forty of them. On asking the market-woman which was right, she replied, "If I had as many more, and one-half as many more, and one-fourth as many more, I should have one short of a hundred. Now puzzle it out for yourselves." What was the number of the flock ?

No. XCVII.—The Divided Cord.

A piece of cord is thirty-six inches in length. Required, so to divide it into two parts that one of them shall be exactly four-fifths the length of the other.

No. XCVIII.—The Divided Number.

Divide the number 46 into two parts in such manner that if the one be divided by 7 and the other by 3, the sum of the quotients shall be 10.

No. XCIX.—The Two Numbers.

There are two numbers, such that twice the first *plus* the second = 17, and twice the second *plus* the first = 19. Find the numbers.

No. C.—The Horse and Trap.

A man purchased a horse and trap. Five times the price of the horse was just equal to twelve times the price of the trap, and the two together cost £85. What was the price of each ?

No. CI.—The Two Workmen.

A, working 7 hours a day, can do a piece of work in 10 days, and *B*, working 8 hours a day, can do it in 7 days. Supposing both employed together, how many hours a day must they work in order to complete it in 5 days ?

No. CII.—Another Divided Number.

Required, to divide the number 237 into three parts, in such manner that 3 times the first shall be equal to 5 times the second and 8 times the third.

No. CIII.—The Three Reapers.

A, *B*, and *C*, working together, can reap a certain field in 5 days. *B*, working alone, would take twice as long as *A* and *C* together; and *C*, working alone, would take three times as long as *A* and *B* together.

How long would each take to do the work separately?

No. CIV.—The Bag of Marbles.

Three boys have a bag of marbles given to them, and it is agreed that they shall be divided in proportion to their ages, which together amount to $17\frac{1}{2}$ years. The bag contains 770 marbles, and as often as Tom takes 4 Jack takes 3, and as often as Tom takes 6 Dick takes 7.

How many marbles will each get, and what are their respective ages?

No. CV.—The Expunged Numerals. A.

Given, the following sum in addition:—

$$111$$
$$777$$
$$999$$

Required, to strike out six of these numbers, so that the total of the remaining numbers shall be 20 only.

No. CVI.—The Expunged Numerals.

Given, the sum following:—

$$111$$
$$333$$
$$555$$
$$777$$
$$999$$

Required, to strike out nine of the above figures, so that the total of the remaining figures shall be 1111.

No. CVII.—A Tradesman in a Difficulty.

A man went into a shop in New York and purchased goods to the amount of 34 cents. When he came to pay, he found that he had only a dollar, a three-cent piece, and a two-cent piece. The tradesman had only a half- and a quarter-dollar. A third man, who chanced to be in the shop, was asked if he could assist, but he proved to have only two dimes, a five-cent piece, a two-cent piece, and a one-cent piece.* With this assistance, however, the shopkeeper managed to give change.

How did he do it?

No. CVIII.—Profit and Loss.

A tradesman sells a parcel of soiled goods at a loss for £2 16s. The market price was £3 5s., at which price he would have made three times as much by them as he actually lost.

What did they cost him originally?

No. CIX.—A Curious Fraction.

What like fractions of a pound, of a shilling, and of a penny will, when added together, make exactly a pound?

No. CX.—The Menagerie.

The proprietor of a menagerie was asked how many birds and how many beasts it included. He replied, "Well, the lot have 36 heads and 100 feet."

How many of each were there?

---

* For the assistance of readers who may not be familiar with the American coinage, we may mention that the cent is equivalent to our halfpenny. Of these 100 go to the dollar, which is therefore worth 4s. 2d., while the half and quarter are equivalent to 2s. 1d. and 1s. 0½d. (50 cents and 25 cents) respectively. The dime is the tenth part of a dollar, and is therefore worth 10 cents, or 5d.

No. CXI.—The Market-woman and her Eggs.

A market-woman, selling eggs, sold to her first customer the half of her stock and half an egg over. To her second customer she sold one-half of the remainder and half an egg over. To a third customer she sold half her yet remaining stock and half an egg over, when she found that she had none left.

How many eggs had she originally ?

No. CXII.—The Cook and his Assistants.

This is a problem of the same kind, differing only in the figures. A cook distributes eggs to his three assistants, to the first one-half and half an egg over, to the second one-half of the remainder and half an egg over, and to the third one-half of what still remains and half an egg over. He has still four eggs left.

How many had he at first ?

KEY TO CHAPTER I.

THE solution of problems of this class is greatly facilitated by an elementary knowledge of the Properties of Numbers. We append, therefore, a statement of some of such properties, not limited to the particular examples we have given (the majority of which depend upon much simpler considerations), but of general utility in relation to such problems. We offer in each case a brief demonstration of the fact stated, though for the purpose of the present work it will be quite sufficient if the reader is content to accept the propositions laid down without demanding mathematical proof of their accuracy.

ELEMENTARY PROPERTIES OF NUMBERS.

PROPOSITION 1.—*The sum or difference of two even numbers is always an even number.*

PROOF.—This becomes self-evident if the proposition be expressed in algebraic form. Thus—

Let $2x$ = the larger number,
and $2y$ = the smaller number.

Then their sum will be $2x + 2y$,
and their difference will be $2x - 2y$;

each of which is obviously divisible by 2, without fraction or remainder—*i.e.*, an even number.

PROP. 2.—*The sum or difference of two odd numbers is always an even number.*

PROOF.—Let $2x + 1$ = the larger number,
and $2y + 1$ = the smaller number.

Then their sum will be $2x + 2y + 2$;
and their difference $2x - 2y$;

each of which is obviously divisible by 2 : *i.e.*, an even number.

PROP. 3.—*The sum of an even and an odd number is always an odd number.*

PROOF.—Let $2x$ = the even number,
and $2y + 1$ = the odd number.

Then their sum will be $2x + 2y + 1$, which is obviously *not* divisible by 2 without a fraction or remainder—*i.e.*, is an odd number.

PROP. 4.—*The difference of an even and an odd number is always an odd number.*

PROOF.—Here there are two possible cases to be considered, as the odd or the even number may be the larger. In the first case—

Let $2x + 1$ = the larger number,
and $2y$ = the smaller number.

Here their difference will be represented by $2x + 1 - 2y$, which is obviously an odd number.

In the second case—
Let $2x$ = the larger number,
and $2y + 1$ = the smaller number.

Then their difference will be represented by $2x - 2y - 1$, which is obviously an odd number.

PROP. 5.—*If the sum of two numbers be an even number, then their difference is also an even number.*

PROOF.—This follows from preceding propositions. The sum of the two numbers being, *ex hypothesi*, even, the numbers themselves must either (by Props. 1, 2, 3) be both even or both odd; and if so, their difference (by Props. 1, 2) must be even.

PROP. 6.—*If the sum of two numbers be an odd number, then their difference is also an odd number.*

PROOF.—This follows from Props. 3 and 4. The sum of the two numbers being odd, the numbers themselves must (by Prop. 3) be one odd, and one even, in which case their difference (by Prop. 4) will be odd.

PROP. 7.—*For a number to be divisible by 2, its last digit must be* EVEN.

PROOF.—(Self-evident. *All odd numbers divided by 2 leave a remainder of* 1.)

PROP. 8.—*If a number to be divisible by* 3, *the sum of its digits will also be divisible by* 3.

PROOF.—Let a represent the units, b the tens, c the hundreds, d the thousands, and so on. Then the whole number may be expressed in the form of a sum in addition, as follows:

$$
\begin{array}{r}
a \\
b\,0 \\
c\,0\,0 \\
d\,0\,0\,0 \\
\hline
d\ c\ b\ a
\end{array}
$$

Now $b\,0 = b\,10 = b\,(9\ +1) = b\,9\ +b$
and $c\,00 = c\,100 = c\,(99\ +1) = c\,99\ +c$
and $d\,000 = d\,1000 = d\,(999+1) = d\,999+d.$
The whole number is therefore equal to

$$
\begin{array}{r}
a \\
b\,9+b \\
c\,99+c \\
d\,999+d
\end{array}
$$

And as $b9 + c99 + d999$ is obviously divisible by 3, it follows that, to make the whole number exactly divisible by 3, $a+b+c+d$ (the sum of its digits), must be divisible by 3 in like manner.

PROP. 9.—*Any number, less the sum of its digits, is divisible by* 3.

PROOF. — This is incidentally proved in the course of the demonstration of Prop. 8, where we have seen that any number may be thrown into the form $b\,9 + c\,99 + d\,999 + a + b + c + d.$ Deducting from this $a + b + c + d$, representing the sum of the digits of the original number, it is clear that the remainder is a multiple of, and therefore divisible by, 3.

PROP. 10.—*Any number, to be exactly divisible by* 4, *must have the number formed by its last two digits divisible by* 4.

PROOF.—Any number of more than two digits consists of so many hundreds as may be expressed by the preceding digits, *plus* the number expressed by the last two digits. (Thus 532 is equivalent to $500+32$; 1429 to $1400+29$, and so on). Each hundred, being a multiple of 4, is necessarily divisible by that number. If, therefore, the remaining digits (the last two) are divisible by 4, the whole number must be so divisible.

PROP. 11.—*For a number to be divisible by 5, it must have either 5 or 0 for its units digit.*

PROOF.—When any given number is divided by 5, the only possible remainder is 0, 1, 2, 3, or 4. Whichever of such remainders be left over from the division up to the *tens* place, it is clear that there must be a 0 or a 5 in the units place to enable the division to be completed without remainder.

PROP. 12.—*For a number to be divisible by 6, it must be an even number, and the sum of its digits must be divisible by 3.*

PROOF.—As $6 = 2 \times 3$, the divisibility of a given number by 6 depends upon its divisibility by 2 and 3; for the tests of which divisibility see Props. 7 and 8.

PROP. 13.—(There is no general criterion as to divisibility by 7.*)

PROP. 14.—*For a number to be evenly divisible by 8, its last three digits must be divisible by 8.*

PROOF.—The proof here follows the same line of argument as that of Prop. 10. Any number of more than three digits consists of a given number of *thousands, plus* the number expressed by the last three digits. Each thousand, being a multiple of 8, is necessarily divisible by 8, and if therefore the number represented by the remaining three digits is divisible by 8, the whole number will be so divisible.

---

* It should, however, be noted that *every cube number* is either exactly divisible by 7, or may be made so by adding or subtracting 1 to or from it.

Prop. 15.—*For a number to be evenly divisible by 9, the sum of its digits must be evenly divisible by 9.*

    Proof.—See the proof of Prop. 8, where it is shown that any given number can be expressed in the form $d\,999 + c\,99 + b\,9 + a + b + c + d$. The portion $d\,999 + c\,99 + b\,9$ being obviously divisible by 9, it follows that to make the whole sum divisible by 9, the remaining portion of the number, $a + b + c + d$ (representing the sum of its digits), must also be divisible by 9.

Prop. 16.—*For a number to be divisible by 10, its last digit must be 0.*

    Proof.—This proposition is practically self-evident. Any given number represents so many tens *plus* the number of units expressed by the last digit. If such last digit be 1, 2, 3, 4, 5, 6, 7, 8, or 9 (*i.e.*, any number save 0), it will represent a remainder of that amount, and the whole number cannot be divided evenly by 10.

Prop. 17.—*The product of any two consecutive numbers (as 4 and 5, 14 and 15, or 26 and 27) is always divisible by 2.*

    Proof.—Of any two consecutive numbers one must be an even number, and therefore a multiple of 2. By whatever other number it may be multiplied, the product will therefore also be divisible by 2.

Prop. 18.—*The product of any three consecutive numbers is always divisible by 6.*

    Proof.—This is demonstrable in like manner, for of three consecutive numbers one must be a multiple of 3, and one of 2*; and if a number is divisible by 3 and by 2, it is also divisible by 6.

Prop. 19.—*The product of any four consecutive numbers is always divisible by 24; of any five, by 120, and so on (the new divisor in each case being obtained by multiplying the last divisor by the number of consecutive figures).*

    Proof.—The proof is a mere extension of that of Prop. 18.

---

* Both characters may be united in the intermediate number, as in the case of 11, 12, 13; 23, 24, 25.

PROP. 20.—*The difference between the squares of two numbers is equal to the product of their sum and difference.*

$$e.g., \quad 5^2 - 3^2 \quad = 25 - 9 = 16$$
$$(5+3) \times (5-3) = 8 \times 2 = 16.$$

PROOF.—This is but a re-statement of the well-known algebraical formula—

$$x^2 - y^2 = (x+y)\ (x-y).$$

But it may be made equally clear without recourse to algebra, thus:—

Take any two numbers—say 5 and 3.

$(5-3)$ multiplied by $(5+3)$ means $(5-3)$ multiplied by 5 and (added on to this) $(5-3)$ multiplied by 3.

Now $(5-3)$ multiplied by 5 gives $5^2 - (5 \times 3)$ and $(5-3)$,, ,, 3 ,, $(5 \times 3) - 3^2$.

Adding the two results together,

$(5-3)$ multiplied by $(5+3) = 5^2 - 3^2$.

And this holds with any numbers, so that generally $n^2 - m^2 = (n+m) \times (n-m)$.

PROP. 21.—*The difference between the squares of any two numbers is always divisible by the difference of the two numbers. It is also divisible by the sum of the two numbers.*

PROOF.—This is a necessary consequence of the preceding proposition.

PROP. 22.—*The difference of the squares of any two odd numbers is always divisible by 8.*

PROOF.—Suppose $(2x+1)$ and $(2y+1)$ to be the two odd numbers.

Then (by Prop. 20) the difference of their squares equals the product of their sum and difference : *i.e.* $(2x+1)^2 - (2y+1)^2 = \{(2x+1) + (2y+1)\} \times \{(2x+1) - (2y+1)\}$

$$= \{2x + 2y + 2\}\{2x - 2y\}$$
$$= 4\{x + y + 1\}\{x - y\}$$

Now if x and y are both odd or both even, then (by Prop. 1) $(x-y)$ is even, in which case $4(x+y+1)\ (x-y)$ is divisible by 4 and further by 2; that is to say, by 8.

But if x and y are unlike,—that is to say one odd and the other even,—then $x+y$ is odd, and therefore $(x+y+1)$ is even; in which case $4(x+y+1)$ $(x-y)$ is again divisible by 4 and further by 2; that is to say, by 8.

Wherefore $(2x+1)^2-(2y+1)^2$ is divisible by 8.

Prop. 23.—*The difference between a number and its cube is the product of three consecutive numbers, and is consequently divisible by 6.*

Suppose n^3 and n to be the cube and the number; then difference between them is n^3-n. This evidently $=n(n^2-1)$.

But looking upon 1 as a square number (the square of unity) we have $(n^2-1)=(n-1)$ $\times(n+1)$, as in Prop. 20.

So that $n^3-n=n(n-1)(n+1)$.

But $(n-1)$, n, and $(n+1)$ are obviously three consecutive numbers, and therefore (by Prop. 18) divisible by 6.

Prop. 24.—*Any prime number which, divided by 4, leaves a remainder 1 is the sum of two square numbers.*

The mathematical proof of the universal truth of this proposition is very complicated, and would be beyond the scope of a work like the present. We subjoin a list of all such numbers below 400, and from the evident truth of the theorem in this large number of cases the reader may be content to infer its general accuracy.

List of all prime numbers below 400 which, being divided by 4, leave a remainder of 1.

$5 =$	$4+ 1 =$	2^2+1^2	$113 =$	$64+ 49 =$	$8^2+ 7^2$
$13 =$	$9+ 4 =$	3^2+2^2	$137 =$	$121+ 16 =$	$11^2+ 4^2$
$17 =$	$16+ 1 =$	4^2+1^2	$149 =$	$100+ 49 =$	$10^2+ 7^2$
$29 =$	$25+ 4 =$	5^2+2^2	$157 =$	$121+ 36 =$	$11^2+ 6^2$
$37 =$	$36+ 1 =$	6^2+1^2	$173 =$	$169+ 4 =$	$13^2+ 2^2$
$41 =$	$25+16 =$	5^2+4^2	$181 =$	$100+ 81 =$	$10^2+ 9^2$
$53 =$	$49+ 4 =$	7^2+2^2	$193 =$	$144+ 49 =$	$12^2+ 7^2$
$61 =$	$36+25 =$	6^2+5^2	$197 =$	$196+ 1 =$	$14^2+ 1^2$
$73 =$	$64+ 9 =$	8^2+3^2	$229 =$	$225+ 4 =$	$15^2+ 2^2$
$89 =$	$64+25 =$	8^2+5^2	$233 =$	$169+ 64 =$	$13^2+ 8^2$
$97 =$	$81+16 =$	9^2+4^2	$241 =$	$225+ 16 =$	$15^2+ 4^2$
$101 =$	$100+ 1 =$	10^2+1^2	$257 =$	$256+ 1 =$	$16^2+ 1^2$
$109 =$	$100+ 9 =$	10^2+3^2	$269 =$	$169+100 =$	13^2+10^2

$277 = 196 + 81 = 14^2 + 9^2$			$349 = 324 + 25 = 18^2 + 5^2$			
$281 = 256 + 25 = 16^2 + 5^2$			$353 = 289 + 64 = 17^2 + 8^2$			
$293 = 289 + 4 = 17^2 + 2^2$			$373 = 324 + 49 = 18^2 + 7^2$			
$313 = 169 + 144 = 13^2 + 12^2$			$389 = 289 + 100 = 17^2 + 10^2$			
$317 = 196 + 121 = 14^2 + 11^2$			$397 = 361 + 36 = 19^2 + 6^2$			
$337 = 256 + 81 = 16^2 + 9^2$						

With this brief introduction we proceed to give the solutions of the various puzzles propounded in the preceding pages.

It is generally very much more easy to solve puzzles of this class by the aid of algebra, and in some instances we have exhibited the solution in this form. But this is scarcely regarded as a legitimate method of solving an arithmetical puzzle, and where the reader can solve such a puzzle by step-by-step argument, without the use of algebraic symbols, he may consider that he has attained a considerably higher measure of success. Even if algebra be used in the first place, the problem should, if possible, be worked out arithmetically afterwards.

No. I.—The Forty-five Puzzle. Solution.

The first of the required numbers is 8.

$$8 + 2 = 10$$

The second is 12.

$$12 - 2 = 10$$

The third is 5.

$$5 \times 2 = 10$$

The fourth is 20.

$$20 \div 2 = 10$$

$$8 + 12 + 5 + 20 = 45.$$

No. II.—A Singular Subtraction. Solution.

This is somewhat of a quibble. The number 45 is the sum of the digits 1, 2, 3, 4, 5, 6, 7, 8, 9. The puzzle is solved by arranging these in reverse order, and subtracting the original series from them, when the remainder will be found to consist of the same digits in a different order, and therefore making the same total—viz., 45.

$$987654321 = 45$$
$$123456789 = 45$$
$$\overline{864197532} = 45$$

No. III.—A Mysterious Multiplicand. Solution.

The number 37 will be found to answer the conditions of the problem. Multiplied by 3, it is 111; by 6, 222; by 9, 333; by 12, 444; by 15, 555; by 18, 666; by 21, 777; by 24, 888; and by 27, 999.

No. IV.—Counting the Pigs. Solution.

Answer.—He had ten.

PROOF: $10 + 10 + 5 + 7 = 32.$

No. V.—Another Pig Problem. Solution.

He had seven.

PROOF: $7 + 7 + 3\frac{1}{2} + 2\frac{1}{2} = 20.$

No. VI.—A Little Miscalculation. Solution.

By the time she has sold 20 lots at 10 for twopence (four of the one kind and six of the other), the 120 cheaper apples are exhausted, while she has only sold 80 of the dearer. So far, she has neither gained nor lost, but she has still on hand 40 of the dearer apples, worth, at cost price, tenpence. By selling these at 10 for twopence she only gets eightpence, leaving a deficit of twopence.

No. VII.—A Simple Magic Square. Solution.

The arrangement depicted in Fig. 338 answers the conditions of the problem, the total being 15 in each direction.

No. VIII.—The Thirty-four Puzzle. Solution.

It is computed that no less than 3456 arrangements of the sixteen figures will answer the required conditions. Whether this total be exact we will not undertake to decide,

2	9	4
7	5	3
6	1	8

Fig. 338.

but it is certain that such arrangements may be numbered by some hundreds. The fact that, with so many possible solutions, they were not oftener hit upon by the hundreds of thousands who, during its temporary "boom," racked their brains over the "Thirty-four" Puzzle arises from the fact that, numerous as they are, they are but as a drop in the ocean compared with the number of combinations (amounting to over twenty billions) of which sixteen given articles are capable.

We append, by way of specimens, a few of the possible solutions (Figs. 339–344).

1	15	14	4
12	6	7	9
8	10	11	5
13	3	2	16

Fig. 339.

1	14	15	4
8	11	10	5
12	7	6	9
13	2	3	16

Fig. 340.

1	12	6	15
13	8	10	3
16	5	11	2
4	9	7	14

FIG. 341.

1	8	15	10
14	11	4	5
12	13	6	3
7	2	9	16

FIG. 342.

1	7	16	10
12	14	5	3
6	4	11	13
15	9	2	8

FIG. 343.

1	11	6	16
8	14	3	9
15	5	12	2
10	4	13	7

FIG. 344.

In each of these cases the number 34 can be counted in ten different directions—viz., four horizontal, four perpendicular, and two diagonal. The simplest method of constructing such squares is as follows :—First arrange the figures (which may be any series in arithmetical progression) in the form of a square in their natural order, as, for example, the series shown in Fig. 345. Regard this as *two* squares, one within the other, as indicated by the heavy black lines. Now re-arrange the series, reversing the diagonals of each such square, when the figures will be as in Fig. 346, counting 46 in each of the directions above-mentioned.

By marshalling, in the first instance, the figures in vertical instead of horizontal rows, the resulting arrangement will be slightly different, but yet producing the same totals (see Figs. 347 and 348).

4	5	6	7
8	9	10	11
12	13	14	15
16	17	18	19

Fig. 345.

19	5	6	16
8	14	13	11
12	10	9	15
7	17	18	4

Fig. 346.

4	8	12	16
5	9	13	17
6	10	14	18
7	11	15	19

Fig. 347.

19	8	12	7
5	14	10	17
6	13	9	18
16	11	15	4

Fig. 348.

Magic squares may, however, be so arranged as to produce the same total in a far greater number of ways. The

1	15	10	8
12	6	3	13
7	9	16	2
14	4	5	11

Fig. 349.

American "34" Puzzle required that the total in question (34) should be produced in twenty different directions.

The problem in such a shape is beyond the scope of any but skilled mathematicians; but our readers may be interested to know that such a result has not only been achieved, but even surpassed, as in the arrangement given in Fig. 349, where 34 is obtained in no less than 24 different ways.

34 may here be counted —

Horizontally	4 ways.
Perpendicularly	4 „
Diagonally	2 „
The four corner squares (1, 8, 14, 11)	1 „
The four centre squares (6, 3, 9, 16)	1 „
The four corner groups of 4 squares, each 1, 15, 12, 6 ; 10, 8, 3, 13 ; 7, 9, 14, 4; and 16, 2, 5, 11 . .	4 „
The four groups of 4 forming the centre of each side—15, 10, 6, 3 ; 12, 6, 7, 9 ; 3, 13, 16, 2 ; and 9, 16, 4, 5 . .	4 „

TOTAL   20 ways.

These are the twenty totals required by the conditions of the American puzzle. But there are yet four other ways in which 34 can be made—viz., by means of adding together the groups on opposite sides of the " octagon "—15, 10, 4, 5 ; 10. 13, 7, 4 ; 13, 2, 12, 7 ; and 12, 15, 5, 2, making in all twenty-four.

Any reader caring to follow the subject further will find much interesting matter in relation to it in a little penny pamphlet published by Heywood of Manchester, entitled *The Curiosities of the Thirty-four Puzzle,* and giving no less than 150 solutions of the problem, with instructions for obtaining the whole number of which it is capable.

No. IX.—The Sixty-Five Puzzle.   Solution.

The arrangement shown in Fig. 350 answers the conditions of the problem, the total being 65 in each direction.

We have given in the last answer the method of forming the simpler magic squares where they consist of an even number of cells. Where the square consists of an odd number of cells, another method is employed. We will take,

in the first place, the simplest possible example: a square
of nine cells, and an arithmetical series * rising by 1 only,
say the numbers 3 to 11 inclusive.

3	20	7	24	11
16	8	25	12	4
9	21	13	5	17
22	14	1	18	10
15	2	19	6	23

FIG. 350.

Having drawn a square of the required number of cells,
add an additional cell on either side, contiguous to the
centre square on that side. It will be seen that this gives
three parallel diagonals, of three squares each, in four
different directions. Arrange your series of numbers in

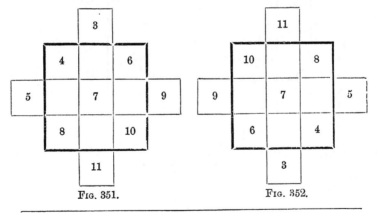

FIG. 351.   FIG. 352.

* It was formerly believed that *only* series of figures in arithmetical
progression were capable of being formed into magic squares; but this
belief has long since been shown to be unfounded.

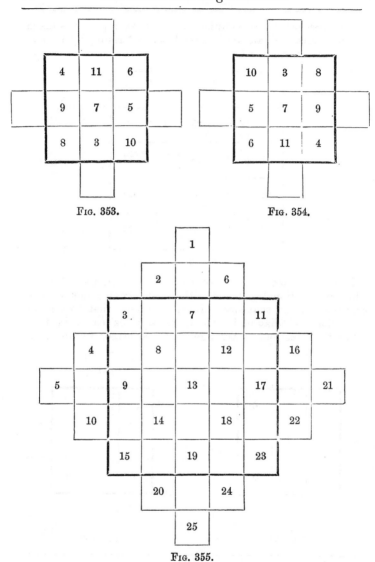

FIG. 353.   FIG. 354.

FIG. 355.

consecutive order in either set of parallels, say as in Fig.
351 or as in Fig. 352.   Then transfer the number in each

external cell to the vacant cell on the opposite side of the square. The respective results will be as shown in Figs. 353 and 354 respectively, either of which will answer the required conditions, giving a total of 21 each way.

With a larger number of cells the process is a little more elaborate, but the principle is the same. Thus, suppose it be required to form a magic square of 25 cells with the numbers 1 to 25 inclusive. We now add extra cells so as to

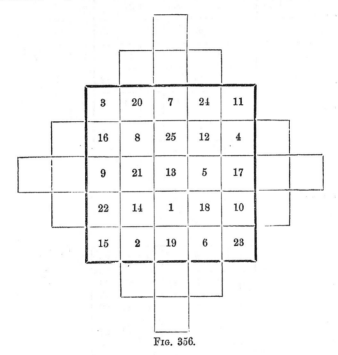

Fig. 356.

form *five* parallel diagonals, as in Fig. 355. Proceeding as before, we arrange the series as shown in the same figure, and then transposing each of the outlying numbers to the vacant square on the opposite side, we have the result shown in Fig. 356, giving a total of 65 each way.

It is to be observed that we have in each case moved the outlying number *five* places onwards, *i.e.* the exact length of one side of the square. Bearing this fact in mind, it becomes

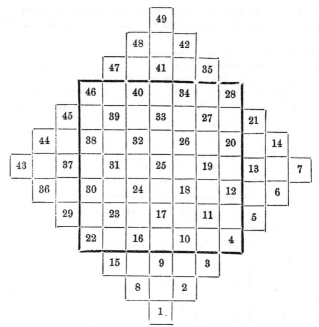

Fig. 357.

46	15	40	9	34	3	28
21	39	8	33	2	27	45
38	14	32	1	26	44	20
13	31	17	25	43	19	37
30	6	24	49	18	36	12
5	23	48	7	42	11	29
22	47	16	41	10	35	4

Fig. 358.

equally easy to deal with squares of a still larger number
of cells (provided always that they consist of an odd

number). Nos. 357 and 358 illustrate the same process as applied to the numbers 1 to 49, arranged to form a magic square of 49 cells, with a total in each direction of 175. (We have in this case started from the bottom, and worked upwards from left to right.) The square in this case having seven cells on a side, each of the outlying figures is moved forward *seven* places, with the result shown in Fig. 358.*

No. X.—The Twenty-Six Puzzle. Solution.

We append, in Figs. 359, 360, two solutions, or varia-

	1	4	
11	6	7	2
8	10	3	5
	9	12	

Fig. 359.

	12	9	
2	7	6	11
5	3	10	8
	4	1	

Fig. 360.

tions of the same solution. It is not impossible that there are many others which would equally answer the conditions of the problem.

No. XI.—An Unmanageable Legacy. Solution.

The lawyer had a horse of his own, which he drove into the stable with the rest. "Now," he said to John, "take your half." John took nine horses accordingly. James and William were then invited to take their shares, which they did, receiving six and two horses respectively. This division exactly disposed of the seventeen horses of the testator; and the lawyer, pocketing his fee, drove his own steed home again.

N.B.—The above solution rests on the fact that the sum of

---

* Further information on the subject of Magic Squares will be found in *Hutton's Mathematical Recreations*, and in the *Encyclopédie des Jeux* of M. de Moulidars, p. 430.

the three fractions named, $\frac{1}{2}$, $\frac{1}{3}$, and $\frac{1}{9}$, when reduced to a common denominator, will be found not to amount to unity, but only to $\frac{17}{18}$. The addition of another horse ($=\frac{1}{18}$) bringing the total number up to eighteen, renders it divisible by such common denominator, and enables each to get his proper share, the lawyer then resuming his own $\frac{1}{18}$, which he had lent for the purpose of the division.

In the administration of the Mahomedan Law of Inheritance, which involves numerous and complicated fractions, this expedient is frequently employed.

No. XII.—Many Figures, but a Small Result. Solution.

$\frac{35}{70} + \frac{148}{296}$.

(Reducing each fraction to its lowest denominator, it will be found to be equal to $\frac{1}{2}$, and $\frac{1}{2} + \frac{1}{2} = 1$.)

No. XIII.—Can You Name it? Solution.

Answer, 20.

$50 - 20 = 30. \quad 80 - 50 = 30.$

No. XIV.—Squares, Product, and Difference. Solution.

Answer, 11 and 15.

Their product is 165, and their difference 4. The former exceeds the latter by 161. The sum of their squares is 346, and $346 - 165 = 181$.

No. XV.—A Peculiar Number. Solution.

The required number is 285714, which, multiplied by 2, becomes 571428.

From the conditions of the question, it is clear that the required number must begin with 28, and end with 14 (one half of 28). As it has six digits, it must therefore take the form 28 .. 14, the two intermediate digits being unknown. It is equally clear that the double number must end with 1428, the last two figures being affixed to the final 14 of the original number. Again, it must begin with either 56 or 57, for any higher number divided by 2 would have a larger quotient than 28, and therefore is by the terms of the problem inadmissible. This gives us as the double number either 561428 or 571428.

Dividing each by 2, we have 280714 and 285714, the second of which is found to answer the required conditions.*

No. XVI.—A Novel Century. Solution.

$9 \times 8 + 7 + 6 + 5 + 4 + 3 + 2 + 1 = 100.$

No. XVII.—Another Century. Solution.

There are several ways of fulfilling the conditions of the puzzle. The first takes the form of a sum in addition:

```
   15
   36
   47
  ───
   98
    2
  ───
  100
```

Other solutions are as follow:

$1\frac{3}{6} + 98\frac{27}{54} + 0 = 100.$ $80\frac{27}{54} + 19\frac{3}{6} = 100.$

$70 + 24\frac{9}{18} + 5\frac{3}{6} = 100.$ $87 + 9\frac{4}{5} + 3\frac{12}{60} = 100.$

No. XVIII.—Another Way to Make 100. Solution.

$99\frac{99}{99}$.

No. XIX.—The Lucky Number. Solution.

Multiply the selected number by *nine*, and use the product as the multiplier for the larger number. It will be found that the results will be respectively as under:—

12345679 ×	9	=	111 111 111
,, ×	18	=	222 222 222
,, ×	27	=	333 333 333
,, ×	36	=	444 444 444
,, ×	45	=	555 555 555
,, ×	54	=	666 666 666
,, ×	63	=	777 777 777
,, ×	72	=	888 888 888
,, ×	81	=	999 999 999

It will be observed that the result is in each case the "lucky" number, nine times repeated.

* See also Puzzle No. XLV.

No. XX.—The Two Ages. Solution.

The father was three times the age of his son $15\frac{1}{2}$ years earlier, being then fifty-five and a half, while his son was eighteen and a half. The son will have reached half his father's age in three years' time, being then thirty-seven, while his father will be seventy-four.

No. XXI.—The Graces and the Muses. Solution.

The number each Grace had originally was 36, for—

She gave to each Muse $\frac{1}{18}$ of her store : *i.e.*, to the nine $\frac{9}{18} = \frac{1}{2}$, leaving $\frac{1}{2}$ still in her own possession ; and each Muse receiving $\frac{1}{18}$ from each Grace, had in all $\frac{3}{18} = \frac{1}{6}$.

But the $\frac{1}{2}$ left to each Grace exceeded the $\frac{1}{6}$ held by each Muse by 12, and if $\frac{1}{2} - \frac{1}{6}$ $(= \frac{1}{3})$ be 12, the whole number must have been 36.

No. XXII.—The Graces and the Muses again. Solution.

Twelve, or any multiple of twelve, will answer the conditions of the puzzle. Assuming the number to be twelve, each Grace gives one rose to each Muse. Each Muse will thus have three (one received from each Grace), while the Graces have each three roses left.

No. XXIII.—Just One Over. Solution.

61, being the least common multiple of 2, 3, 4, 5, and 6 (60) + 1.

No. XXIV.—Scarcely Explicit. Solution.

He had £20, as may be seen by the following demonstration :—

Let x be the number of pounds in his pocket. Then, according to the conditions of the puzzle,

$$x + \tfrac{1}{2}x + \tfrac{2}{3}x + \tfrac{3}{4}x + \tfrac{4}{5}x + \tfrac{5}{6}x + 9 = 100$$

Reducing the fractions to a common denominator :

$$x + \left(\frac{30 + 40 + 45 + 48 + 50}{60} \right) x = 100 - 9$$

i.e.
$$x + \frac{213x}{60} \left(= x + \frac{71}{20} x \right) = 91$$

$$\frac{20x + 71x}{20} = 91$$

$$\frac{91x}{20} = 91$$

$$\frac{x}{20} = 1$$

$$x = 20$$

No. XXV.—Making Things Even. Solution.

Johnny had sevenpence, and Tommy fivepence.

No. XXVI.—A Rejected Proposal. Solution.

Johnny had eightpence, and Tommy fourpence.

No. XXVII.—The Market Woman and her Stock. Solution.

Her original stock was 40 apples. Her first customer, buying half her stock, and giving back 10, left her with 30; the second, buying one-third of 30, and giving her back 2, left her with 22; and the third, buying half of these, and giving her back 1, left her with 12.

To solve the problem, however, it is necessary (unless algebra be used) to work the process backwards. Take away 1 (given back by the last boy) from her ultimate remainder, 12, thus leaving 11. It is clear that as he purchased half her stock, she must before he did so have had 22 apples. Of these, 2 had been given back to her by the second boy, so that prior to his so doing she must have had 20. As he bought one-third of her stock, the number previous to his purchase must have been 30. Of these 30, 10 were given back to her by the first boy, prior to which she must have had 20; and as this 20 represents half her original stock (for the first boy bought the other half), she must at the outset have had 40.

No. XXVIII.—The Captives in the Tower.   Solution.

The boy descended first, using the cannon-ball as a counter-poise.   The queen and her daughter then took the cannon-ball out of the upper basket, and the daughter descended, the boy acting as counterpoise.   The cannon-ball was then allowed to run down alone.   When it reached the ground, the daughter got into the basket along with the cannon-ball, and their joint weight acted as counterpoise while the queen descended.   The princess got out, and the cannon-ball was sent down alone.   The boy then went down, the cannon-ball ascending.   The daughter removed the cannon-ball and went down alone, her brother ascending.   The latter then put the cannon-ball in the opposite basket, and lowered himself to the ground.

No. XXIX.—Father and Son.   Solution.

In four years and a half, when the son will be sixteen and a half, the father forty-nine and a half.   When the son reaches 16, the father will be 49—*i.e.*, still a little more than three times the son's age.   But when the son reaches 17, his father will be 50, which is not quite three times 17.   It is, therefore, clear that the required age is between those two points, and a little reflection will show that only the ages stated exactly answer the conditions of the problem.

No. XXX.—A Complicated Transaction.   Solution.

William had 48 shillings, and Thomas 30.

The arithmetical solution of this question is somewhat intricate, but by the algebraic method it is simple enough.

Thus: Let w = William's number,

and t = Thomas' number.

Then the state of William's finances at the close of the transaction will be represented by $w - t + (w - t)$, and by the terms of the question this = 36.   We also have it stated in the question that the joint finances $w + t = 36 + 42 = 78$, so that $w = 78 - t$.

Reducing the first equation to simpler form, we have

$$2w - 2t = 36$$
$$\text{or } w - t = 18$$
$$\text{and } w = 18 + t$$

Comparing the values of w thus ascertained, we have
$$18 + t = 78 - t$$
$$2t = 78 - 18 = 60$$
$$\therefore t = 30$$
and w being $= 18 + t = 18 + 30 = 48$.

No. XXXI.—A Long Family. Solution.

Their respective ages are as follows: the youngest 3, and the eldest 24.

Here again the assistance of algebra is needed for a ready solution.

Let $x =$ the age of the youngest (fifteenth). Then $8x =$ the age of the eldest.

And by the terms of the question—

$8x = (x + 1\frac{1}{2} + 1\frac{1}{2} + 1\frac{1}{2} + 1\frac{1}{2} + 1\frac{1}{2} + 1\frac{1}{2} + 1\frac{1}{2} + 1\frac{1}{2}$
$+ 1\frac{1}{2} + 1\frac{1}{2} + 1\frac{1}{2} + 1\frac{1}{2} + 1\frac{1}{2} + 1\frac{1}{2} = x + 21.$

i.e. $7x = 21$.

$\therefore x = 3$: the age of the youngest,
and $8x = 24$: the age of the eldest.

No. XXXII.—A Curious Number. Solution.

This problem seems at first sight somewhat formidable, but it is in reality very easy.

It is susceptible of various answers, equally correct, according to the value assigned to the smallest part, or unit of measurement. Thus, if such smallest part be 1, the number will be
$$1 + 40 + 400 + 500 = 941$$

If such unit be 2, the number will be
$$2 + 80 + 800 + 1000 = 1882$$

and so on, *ad infinitum*.

No. XXXIII.—The Shepherd and his Sheep.

To ascertain the number of the flock, find in the first place the least common multiple of 2, 3, 4, 5, and 6—*i.e.*, 60. Then take the lowest multiple of this, which, with 1 added, will be divisible by 7. This will be found to be 301, which is the required answer.*

---

* See also answer to No. L.

No. XXXIV.—A Difficult Problem.   Solution.

The solution of this problem depends upon certain of the Properties of Numbers referred to at the commencement of this section (see pp. 174–181), where we find it stated that the condition that a number shall be evenly divisible by—

(I.) 2, is that its last digit shall be an even number. (Prop. 7.)

(II.) 3, is that the sum of its digits shall be divisible by 3. (Prop. 8.)

(III.) 4, is that its last two digits shall be divisible by 4. (Prop. 10.)

(IV.) 5, is that it shall end with 5 or 0.   (Prop. 11.)

(V.) 6, is that the sum of its digits shall be divisible by 3, and its last digit be an even number. (Prop. 12.)

(VI.) 8, is that its last three digits shall be divisible by 8. (Prop. 14.)

(VII.) 9, is that the sum of its digits shall be divisible by 9. (Prop. 15.)

(VIII.) 10, is that its last digit shall be 0.* (Prop. 16.)

To find the required number, let a be the digit occupying the "units" place, b the digit occupying the "tens" place, c that occupying the "hundreds" place, d the "thousands," and so on, as far as may be necessary.

Now, bearing in mind the conditions of the problem, we are enabled at once to fix the value of a. As the required number when divided by 2 is to leave a remainder of 1, we know (by I.) that a must be an even number + 1—*i.e.*, an *odd* number. As the required number is to be divisible by 5, with a remainder of 4, a must (by IV.) be 5 + 4 *or* 0 + 4—*i.e.*, 9 or 4. But as it is to be divisible by 10, with remainder 9, it can only (by VIII.) be 0 + 9 = 9.

From III. we gather that the required number being divisible by 4, with remainder 3, $b\,a$ must be a multiple

---

* Some of these conditions might in the actual working out of the problem be disregarded—*e.g.*, if a number be divisible by 8, with remainder 7, it will, as a matter of course, be divisible by 4, with remainder 3, or by 2, with remainder 1. If divisible by 6, with remainder 5, it will necessarily be divisible by 3, with remainder 2 ; and if divisible by 10, with remainder 9, it will in like manner be divisible by 5, with remainder 4.

of 4, + 3. As $a = 9$, $a - 3$ must $= 6$, and such multiple of 4 must therefore be one ending with 6. Now of such multiples (consisting of two digits only) there are but five—viz., 16, 36, 56, 76, and 96. $b\,a$ must therefore be one or other of these + 3: *i.e.*, either 19, 39, 59, 79, or 99. But neither of these standing alone answers the remaining conditions of the problem. The required number must therefore be one of more than two digits, terminating with one or other of the double numbers above-mentioned.

As the required number is divisible by 9, with remainder 8, we know (by VII.) that the sum of its digits, *less* 8, must be exactly divisible by 9. Deducting 8 from each of the five possible values of $b\,a$, we have as remainders 11, 31, 51, 71, and 91; the sum of whose digits is 2, 4, 6, 8, and 10 respectively. If, therefore, the required number be one of three figures, c must be either $9 - 2 = 7$; $9 - 4 = 5$; $9 - 6 = 3$; $9 - 8 = 1$; *or* $18 - 10 = 8$; and $c\,b\,a$ must be either 719, 539, 359, 179, or 899.

Neither of these, however, is divisible by 7, with remainder 6; and it is therefore clear that no number of three digits only will answer the required conditions.

Proceeding to the consideration of numbers of four digits, we naturally begin with such as have 1 as the value of d. Now (by VII.) we know that, to answer the required conditions, $(1 + c + b + a)$ must be a multiple of 9, with 8 over; or, substituting the known value of a, we have

$$1 + c + b + 9 = (9 \text{ or } 18)* + 8$$
$$= 17 \text{ or } 26$$
$$\therefore\ c + b = 7 \text{ or } 16$$

And as we already know that b is either 1, 3, 5, 7, or 9, c must be either 6, 4, 2, 0, or 7. The only possible solutions commencing with 1 are therefore 1619, 1439, 1259, 1079, or 1799. Of these, however, none save 1259 is divisible by 7, with 6 over, and this number is not divisible by 8, with 7 over.

We proceed to try 2 as the value of d. Then, as before:

$$2 + c + b + a = (9 \text{ or } 18) + 8$$
$$2 + c + b + 9 = 17 \text{ or } 26$$
$$c + b = 6 \text{ or } 15$$

---

* 18 is the highest possible multiple of 9 that will suit the equation. For, even supposing the unknown values of c and b to be each 9, $1 + 9 + 9 + 9$ would obviously not $= 27$ (the next highest multiple) $+ 8$.

in which case, b being known to be either 1, 3, 5, 7, or 9,
c must be either 5, 3, 1, 8, or 6, and the only possible solutions commencing with 2 are—

2519, 2339, 2159, 2879, and 2699.

Of these, 2519 is the only one which answers all the conditions of the problem, and 2519 is therefore the required
number.

No. XXXV.—Well Laid Out. Solution.

Either of the solutions following will answer the conditions
of the problem :—

		s.	d.
2 pieces indiarubber	@ 4d. =		8
2 sheets of paper...	@ 3d. =		6
1 pencil	@ 2d. =		2
16 drawing-pins ...	@ ½d. =		8
21 articles.	Cost	2.	0

		s.	d.
or, 5 pencils	@ 2d. =		10
1 sheet of paper....	@ 3d. =		3
1 piece indiarubber	@ 4d. =		4
14 drawing-pins ...	@ ½d. =		7
21 articles.	Cost	2.	0

To arrive at the result we, in the first place, consider
what one article of each kind would together amount to.
The result is as under :—

1 piece indiarubber	@ 4d.
1 sheet of paper ...	@ 3d.
1 pencil	@ 2d.
1 drawing-pin ...	@ ½d.
4	9½

We have thus only *four* articles (less than one-fifth of the
required number), for 9½d., which is more than one-third of
the total sum to be expended. It is therefore clear that to
make up the total of 21 articles a considerable proportion,
numerically, must be pins; and it is further clear that, to

avoid an odd halfpenny in the total, the number of pins must of necessity be *even*.

We proceed to try one of each of the three more costly articles (value 4*d.* + 3*d.* + 2*d.* = 9*d.*), with such a number of pins as will bring the total number nearer to the required 21. 18 would bring it to exactly that number, but the cost would be only 9*d.* + 9*d.* = 1*s.* 6*d.*; so that the quantity of the cheaper items (the pins) is obviously now in excess. With 16 pins we have 3 + 16 = 19 articles, value 1*s.* 5*d.* This is 2 articles and 7 pence short of the limit. We have therefore to consider what 2 additional articles would together represent 7*d.* in value, and we find that a second piece of rubber, value 4*d.*, and a second sheet of paper, value 3*d.*, just answer the required conditions. This leads us to the first of the solutions above given.

But we have further to consider whether this is the *only* solution—and we accordingly proceed to try 14 drawing-pins (value 7*d.*), with one of each of the other articles. This gives us a total of 17 articles, value 1*s.* 4*d.* This is 8*d.* short in value, and 4 short in number of the required result. The only 4 articles that would make up the required value are 4 additional pencils. Adding these, and their value, we have the second solution.

We proceed to try whether the required conditions can be answered with *twelve* pins, and one of each of the more costly articles. This gives us 15 articles, value 1*s.* 3*d.*, being 6 short in number, and 9*d.* short in value. Now, 6 pencils (the cheapest of the more costly articles) would cost 1*s.*, being 3*d.* in excess of our limit in price; and any further diminution of the number of drawing-pins would bring us still more in excess of such limit. It follows that the above-mentioned are the only possible solutions.

No. XXXVI.—The Two Travellers. Solution.

A, in his 2½ hours' start, has travelled 10 miles. As *B* gains on him at the rate of a mile an hour, it will take him ten hours to recover this distance, by which time *A* will have been travelling 12½ hours, and will be 50 miles from the point whence he started.

No. XXXVII.—Measuring the Garden. Solution.

The garden is 111 yards long by 37 wide, and contains, therefore, 4107 square yards. If it were a yard more each way (112 yards by 38) its area would be 4256 square yards. $4256 - 4107 = 149$.

The problem may be solved algebraically as follows :—

Let x = breadth in yards
Then $3x$ = length ,,
And $3x^2$ = area.

And $(x+1)(3x+1) = (3x^2 + 4x + 1)$ = area if length and breadth increased by one yard each way.

By the terms of the question, such last-mentioned area—

$$3x^2 + 4x + 1 = 3x^2 + 149$$
$$4x + 1 = 149$$
$$i.e., \; 4x = 148$$
$$\therefore \; x = 37 \text{ the required breadth.}$$
$$\text{and } 3x = 141 \text{ ,, length.}$$

No. XXXVIII.—When Will They Get It? Solution.

In 420 days; 420 being the least common multiple of 1, 2, 3, 4, 5, 6, and 7.

No. XXXIX.—Passing the Gate. Solution.

He had at the outset five shillings and one penny.

On the first day he pays one penny at the gate, spends half a crown, and pays a penny on going out, leaving him with two and fivepence.

The second day he pays a penny on entering, spends fourteen-pence, and after paying a penny on going out is left with thirteenpence.

The third day he brings in one shilling, spends sixpence, and is left, on going out, with fivepence.

The fourth day he brings in fourpence, spends twopence, and after paying the toll to go out, is left with one penny only.

To solve the problem, the calculation must be worked backwards. Thus, on the fourth day he pays a penny on coming out, and has still one left, together making twopence. He had spent *half* his available money in the town. The total must therefore on that day have been fourpence, exclusive of the penny he paid to come in. This gives us fivepence as the amount with which he came out the previous evening. The penny he paid to get out brings this amount to sixpence, and as he had first spent a like amount, he must previously have had a shilling, exclusive of the penny to come in.

By continuing the same process, it is easy to arrive at his original capital.

No XL.—A Novel Magic Square. Solution.

(See Fig. 361.) This is an interesting example of what is called the "bordered" magic square, the repeated removal of the border not affectiug its magic quality. The sums of the various rows are 369, 287, 205, and 123, of which the central number, 41, is the greatest common divisor. As to the

5	80	59	73	61	3	63	12	13
1	20	55	30	57	29	71	26	81
4	14	31	50	29	60	35	68	78
76	58	46	38	45	40	36	24	6
7	63	33	43	41	39	49	17	75
74	64	48	42	37	44	34	18	8
67	10	47	32	53	22	51	72	15
66	56	27	52	25	54	11	62	16
69	2	23	9	21	79	19	70	77

Fig. 361.

mode of constructing such squares, see *Hutton's Mathematical Recreations*, and other works of the same kind.

We append, for the purpose of comparison (Fig. 362), the ordinary magic square of the numbers 1 to 81, constructed according to the rule given on pp. 187–189. It will be seen that this, though perfect as an ordinary magic square, wholly fails to meet the special conditions of the problem. The total of each row is in this case 369.

5	54	13	62	21	70	29	78	37
46	14	63	22	71	30	79	38	6
15	55	23	72	31	80	39	7	47
56	24	64	32	81	40	8	48	16
25	65	33	73	41	9	49	17	57
66	34	74	42	1	50	18	58	26
35	75	43	2	57	10	59	27	67
76	44	3	52	11	60	19	68	36
45	4	53	12	61	20	69	28	77

Fig. 362.

No. XLI.—Another Magic Square.   Solution.

45	17	58	6	55	11	32	28
10	54	29	33	16	44	7	59
23	43	0	60	13	49	26	38
48	12	39	27	42	22	61	1
62	2	41	21	36	24	51	15
25	37	14	50	3	63	20	40
4	56	19	47	30	34	9	53
35	31	52	8	57	5	46	18

Fig. 363.

The solution is as shown in Fig. 363. This is a very pretty example of what is known to mathematicians as the Tesselated Magic Square.*

No. XLII.—The Set of Weights. Solution.

The five weights are as under :—

$\frac{1}{2}$ lb., 1$\frac{1}{2}$ lb., 4$\frac{1}{2}$ lbs., 13$\frac{1}{2}$ lbs., and 40$\frac{1}{2}$ lbs.

To weigh the intermediate quantities from 1 lb. upwards, the weights are distributed between the two scales as follows :—

	In Weight Scale.	In Goods Scale.
To weigh 1 lb.	1$\frac{1}{2}$ lb. weight	The goods to be weighed plus $\frac{1}{2}$ lb. weight.
„ 2 lbs.	1$\frac{1}{2}$ and $\frac{1}{2}$ lb. weight.	Goods only.
„ 2$\frac{1}{2}$ „	4$\frac{1}{2}$ lb weight.	Goods $+1\frac{1}{2}$ and $\frac{1}{2}$ lbs.
„ 3 „	4$\frac{1}{2}$ „	Goods $+1\frac{1}{2}$ lb.
„ 5 „	4$\frac{1}{2}$ and $\frac{1}{2}$ lb „	Goods only.
„ 5$\frac{1}{2}$ „	4$\frac{1}{2}$ and 1$\frac{1}{2}$ lb. „	Goods $+\frac{1}{2}$ lb.
„ 6 „	4$\frac{1}{2}$ and 1$\frac{1}{2}$ lb. „	Goods only.
„ 6$\frac{1}{2}$ „	4$\frac{1}{2}$,1$\frac{1}{2}$,and $\frac{1}{2}$ „	„
„ 7 „	13$\frac{1}{2}$ lb. „	Goods, 4$\frac{1}{2}$,1$\frac{1}{2}$,and $\frac{1}{2}$ lbs.
„ 7$\frac{1}{2}$ „	13$\frac{1}{2}$ lb. „	„ 4$\frac{1}{2}$ and 1$\frac{1}{2}$ lbs.
„ 8 „	13$\frac{1}{2}$ and $\frac{1}{2}$ lb. „	„ 4$\frac{1}{2}$ and 1$\frac{1}{2}$ lbs.
„ 8$\frac{1}{2}$ „	13$\frac{1}{2}$ lb. „	„ 4$\frac{1}{2}$ and $\frac{1}{2}$ lbs.
„ 9 „	13$\frac{1}{2}$ lb. „	„ 4$\frac{1}{2}$ lbs.

And so on ; to weigh 60 lbs., all of the weights, with the exception of the $\frac{1}{2}$ lb., being placed in the weight scale.

N.B.—If preferred, the weighing of any given quantity up to 60 lbs. with the weights named may be propounded as an independent puzzle.

No. XLIII.—What Did He Lose? Solution.

The reply of most people is, almost invariably, that the hatter lost £3 19s. 0d. and the value of the hat, but a little consideration will show that this is incorrect. His actual

---

* We are indebted for this particular Magic Square to a recent issue (May 13th, 1893) of the *Queen*, where it appears in connection with a more than ordinarily complex example of the Knight's Tour Puzzle.

loss was £3 19s. 0d., *less* his trade profit on the hat; the nett value of the hat, *plus* such trade profit, being balanced by the difference, 21s., which he retained out of the proceeds of the note.

No. XLIV.—A Difficult Division. Solution.

According to the conditions of the problem, each son's share will be seven casks (irrespective of contents), and of wine, 3½ casks.

The division can be made in either of two ways, as under :—

Dick and Tom each take 2 full, 2 empty, and 3 half-full casks; and

Harry, 3 full, 3 empty, and 1 half-full ;

or

Dick and Tom each take 3 full, 3 empty, and 1 half-full cask; and Harry 1 full, 1 empty, and 5 half-filled casks.

No. XLV.—The Hundred Bottles of Wine. Solution.

He sold on the first day 2 bottles only; on the second, 5 ; on the third, 8; on the fourth, 11; on the fifth, 14; on the sixth, 17 ; on the seventh, 20 ; and on the eighth day, 23.

$$2 + 5 + 8 + 11 + 14 + 17 + 20 + 23 = 100$$

To ascertain the first day's sale, or first term of the series, take the ordinary formula for ascertaining the sum of an arithmetical progression.

$$S = \frac{n}{2}(2a + \overline{n-1b})$$

Now S (the sum of the series), n (the number of terms), and b (the daily rate of increase), are known, being 100, 8, and 3 respectively.   Substituting these known values in the formula, that of the first term, a, is readily ascertained. Thus :—

$$
\begin{aligned}
100 &= \tfrac{8}{2}(2a + 21) \\
&= 4(2a + 21) \\
&= 8a + 84 \\
100 - 84 &= 8a \\
16 &= 8a \\
a &= 2
\end{aligned}
$$

No. XLVI.—**The Last of her Stock. Solution.**

She had 14, of which Willie got 8 (7 + 1); Tommy, 4 (3 + 1) ; and Jennie, 2 (1 + 1).

No. XLVII.—**The Walking Match. Solution.**

They will meet in an hour, by which time A will have gone round the circle exactly five times, B four times, C three times, and D twice.

No. XLVIII.—**A Feat of Divination. Solution.**

All that is necessary is to deduct 25 from the final sum named. This will give a remainder of two figures, representing the points of the two dice.

Thus, suppose that the points thrown are 6 and 1, and that the thrower selects the former to be multiplied. The figures will then be as follows:—

$$(6 \times 2 + 5) \times 5 + 1 = 86$$
$$86 - 25 = 61$$

which, as will be seen, corresponds with the points of the two dice.

If the thrower had selected the 1 as the starting-point of the process, the only difference in the result would be that the two digits would come out in reverse order. Thus:—

$$(1 \times 2 + 5) \times 5 + 6 = 41$$
$$41 - 25 = 16$$

The same process, in a slightly modified form, is equally applicable to three dice. In this case the steps are as under :—

Multiply the points of the first die by 2 ;
Add 5 ;
Multiply the result by 5 ;
Add the points of the second die.
Multiply the total by 10 ;
Add the points of the third die ;
On the final result being announced, the operator subtracts from it 250, when the remainder will give the points of the three dice.

Thus, suppose the points of the three dice to be 5, 4, and 2. Then—

$$5 \times 2 + 5 = 15$$
$$15 \times 5 = 75$$
$$75 + 4 = 79$$
$$79 \times 10 = 790$$
$$790 + 2 = 792$$

And $792 - 250 = 542$, giving the three numbers required.

No. XLIX.—A Peculiar Number. Solution.

The required number is 142,857, which, if multiplied by 5, is 714,285 ; if multiplied by 3, is 428,571 ; or, if multiplied by 6, is 857,142.*

Formidable as the problem may appear, the result is readily obtained by means of a simple equation, as follows :—

The figure which occupies the units place in the original number being 7, let $x =$ the remaining part of the number (the other five digits). Then $10x + 7$ will be the required number. When the 7 is transposed to the left-hand end of the row, the new number will be represented by $700,000 + x$, and by the terms of the problem this latter number is five times the former, i.e.—

$$700,000 + x = 5\,(10x + 7)$$
$$= 50x + 35$$
$$\text{Or } 49x = 700,000 - 35 = 699,965$$
$$\text{Then } x = 14,285$$
$$\text{And } 10x + 7 = 142,857\text{—the required number.}$$

Multiplication by 3 and by 6 proves that this number also answers the remaining conditions.

No. L.—Another Peculiar Number. Solution.

Answer, 121.

To discover the required number in questions of this class, find the least common multiple of all but the number which divides without remainder. Add 1 to such L.C.M., and see whether the result answers the further condition of the problem—i.e., equal division by the remaining number.

If not, multiply the L.C.M. by 2, 3, 4, and so on in succession, each time adding 1, till you obtain a result which is evenly divisible by such number.

---

* For other peculiarities of this number, *see* Puzzle XV.

Applying this rule to the question under consideration, we find that the L.C.M. of 2, 3, 4, 5 and 6 is 60; but 60 + 1 (= 61) is not evenly divisible by 11. We proceed to try 60 × 2 + 1 (= 121), which is found to be so divisible, and is therefore the number required.

No. LI.—The Three Legacies. Solution.

As the amount of each share is to correspond with length of service, it is plain that the housemaid will receive one share, the parlourmaid three, and the cook six—in all, ten shares. The value of a single share is therefore one-tenth of £70, or £7, which is the portion of the housemaid, the parlourmaid receiving £21, and the cook £42.

No. LII.—Another Mysterious Multiplicand. Solution.

The conditions of the problem are answered by the number 73, which, being multiplied by 3, 6, and 9, the products are 219, 438, and 657 respectively. The correctness of the solution is obvious. The rationale of the fact and the process whereby the required number is ascertained, we must confess ourselves unable to explain.

No. LIII.—How to Divide Twelve among Thirteen.

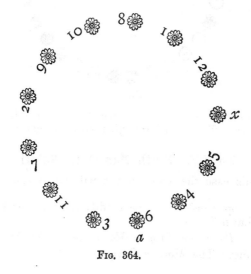

Fig. 364.

It will be found that, counting as described in the problem, the person standing *eleventh* from the point at which you begin will be excluded. The distributor will therefore begin ten places farther back, or (which is the same thing) three places farther forward, in the circle. Thus, if x (see Fig. 364) be the person to be excluded, the distributor will begin to count at the point a. The numbers placed against the various places show the order in which the gifts will be distributed and the men drop out of the circle.

No. LIV.—Tenth Man Out. Solution.

The arrangement was as shown in Fig. 365, the white

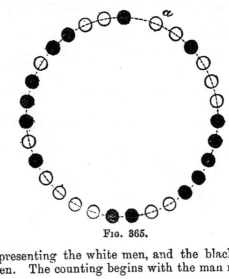

FIG. 365.

spots representing the white men, and the black spots the black men. The counting begins with the man marked a.

No. LV.—Ninth Man Out. Solution.

In this case the arrangement will be as shown in Fig. 366.

The proper order may be readily remembered by the aid of the Latin line—

Populeam Virgam Mater Regina Ferebat,

signifying, "The Mother Queen carried a poplar switch."

The interpretation has, however, nothing to do with the matter. The significance of the formula lies in the *vowels*

FIG. 366.

which occur in it, and which are taken to mean—*a*, 1; *e*, 2; *i*, 3; *o*, 4; and *u*, 5, respectively. The line, therefore, to the initiated, reads as under :—

Po-pu-le-am Vir-gam Ma-ter Re-gi-na Fe-re-bat;
4 5 21 3 1   1 2   2 3 1 2 2 1

which will be found to correspond with the grouping of whites and blacks around the circle. Thus, the *o* in *Po* indicates that the first group is to consist of 4 whites, the *u* in *pu* that the next group is to consist of 5 blacks, and so on, black and white alternately throughout.

No. LVI.—The Three Travellers. Solution.

The plan adopted is as follows :—

1. Two of the servants are sent over.

2. One of the servants brings back the boat, and takes over the third servant.

3. One of the servants brings the boat back, lands, and two of the masters go over.

4. One of the masters and one of the servants return. The servant lands, and the third master crosses with the second.

The position of matters is now as follows: The three

masters are on the farther side, and one of the servants, who is sent back with the boat, and fetches, one at a time, the other two servants.*

No. LVII.—The Wolf, the Goat, and the Cabbages. Solution.

This is a very simple problem.   It is solved as under :—

1. He first takes across the goat, and leaves him on the opposite side.

2. He returns and fetches the wolf, leaves him on the opposite side, and takes back the goat with him.

3. He leaves the goat at the starting-point, and takes over the basket of cabbages.

4. He leaves the cabbages with the wolf, and returning, fetches the goat.

Or,

1. He takes over the goat.

2. He returns and fetches the cabbages.

3. He takes back the goat, leaves him at the starting-point, and fetches the wolf.

4. He leaves the wolf on the opposite side with the basket of cabbages, and goes back to fetch the goat.

No. LVIII.—The Three Jealous Husbands.   Solution.

For the sake of clearness, we will designate the three husbands *A*, *B*, and *C*, and their wives, *a*, *b*, and *c*, respectively.   The passage may then be made to the satisfaction of the husbands in the following order :—

1. *a* and *b* cross over, and *b* brings back the boat.

2. *b* and *c* cross over, *c* returning alone.

---

* It will be found a great advantage in this class of puzzles to have some material representative of each character.   This requirement is met by Messrs. Jaques & Son in the present case by a little mechanical arrangement, under the name of " The Boat Puzzle."   A little boat is mounted on a grooved board, representing the stream, while the masters and servants are represented by six movable figures, three white and three black.

For lack of such an appliance, counters or cardboard discs, with the names of the various persons or objects written upon them, will be found useful.

3. *c* lands, and remains with her husband, while *A* and *B* cross over. *A* lands, *B* and *b* return to the starting-point.

4. *B* and *C* cross over, leaving *b* and *c* at the starting-point.

5. *a* takes back the boat, and *b* crosses with her.

6. *a* lands, and *b* goes back for *c*.

Arithmeticians have racked their brains to devise a means of transit for four husbands and four wives under like conditions, but, with a boat holding two persons only, the problem is insoluble. If we suppose, however, that the boat contains three persons, it may be solved as follows :—

(Distinguishing the four husbands as *A*, *B*, *C*, and *D*, and the four wives as *a*, *b*, *c*, and *d*, respectively.)

1. *a*, *b*, and *c* cross over ; *c* brings back the boat.

2. *c* and *d* cross over, and *d* brings back the boat.

3. *A*, *B*, and *C* cross over ; *C* and *c* bring back the boat.

4. *C*, *D*, and *c* cross over.

5. *c* takes back the boat and fetches *d*.

No. LIX.—The Captain and his Company. Solution.

The captain orders the two children to pass to the farther side. One of them then brings back the boat, lands, and a soldier crosses alone to the farther side. The second child then brings back the boat.

The state of things (save that one man has crossed) is now just as at first, the boat and the two children being on the hither side of the stream. The process is repeated until the whole of the company have passed over.

No. LX.—The Treasure Trove. Solution.

The secret lies in the fact that the process indicated by the Scotchman simply brings back the number with which it started ; *i.e.*, the number of coins in the "find," as will be seen by the following demonstration. Let us suppose x to be the unknown number. Then $x + 666$ will represent the result of the first step; $999 - (x + 666)$ *or* $333 - x$ that of the second step ; and $333 - (333 - x) = x$ that of the third step.

The real value of x is, throughout, unknown to the Scotchman ; but the Irishman, finding that the suggested process has brought out the required amount, rashly assumes that his antagonist must be acquainted with it.

No. LXI.—The Row of Counters. Solution.

The required number will be the original difference *plus* the number removed, at the second stage of the puzzle, from the smaller row ; in this case, therefore, $3 + 5 (= 8)$. This result will be correct whatever were the actual numbers of the two rows originally. This may be illustrated algebraically as follows :—

Let $x =$ number in larger row,
$\quad\quad y = \quad$ „   „   smaller row,
and $R =$ ultimate remainder of larger row.

As the difference of the two rows is stated to be 3, it follows that $x = y + 3$.

And the smaller row, after deduction of the special number indicated, which we will call z, will be $y - z$, and R, the ultimate remainder of the larger row, after deduction of $y - z$, will be $x - (y-z)$, or $x + z - y$.

Substituting for x the value above found, we have

$$R = (y+3) + z - y$$
$$= 3 + z$$

And z being a known number (in this case 5); $R = 8$; or, in other words, the original difference *plus* the number removed from the smaller row prior to the second deduction.

An example may render the process clearer. Thus, suppose that the first row consists of eighteen, and the second of thirteen counters. The difference is in such case 5. Subtract what number you please, say 7, from the smaller row. This leaves 6. 6 being subtracted from 18, the number of the larger row, the remainder will be 12. $(5 + 7)$.

No. LXII.—A Loan and a Present. Solution.

The remainder in this case will be one half of the amount added by way of "present." This is very easily demonstrated.

Let x equal the number thought of; then $2x + 14$ will equal that number *plus* the imaginary loan and present. Half that amount being professedly given to the poor, will leave a remainder of $x + 7$, and on the repayment of the imaginary loan the figures will stand as $x + 7 - x (= 7)$, the value of x having no bearing whatever on the result.

No. LXIII.—Eleven Guests in Ten Beds. Solution.

The fallacy lies in the fact that the real eleventh man remains unprovided with a resting-place. The tenth man having taken possession of the ninth bed, the eleventh man should in due course occupy the tenth bed, but he does not do so. The man who is called from sleeping double in the first bed to occupy this is not the eleventh, but the second man, and the real eleventh man goes bedless.

No. LXIV.—A Difficult Division. Solution.

	8 gal.	5 gal.	3 gal.
1. They begin by filling the five-gallon from the eight-gallon measure. The contents of the three vessels are then—	3 „	5 „	0 „
2. They fill the three gallons from the five gallons, making—	3 „	2 „	3 „
3. They empty the three gallons into the eight-gallon measure	6 „	2 „	0 „
4. They empty the two gallons from the five-gallon into the three-gallon measure	6 „	0 „	2 „
5. They fill the five-gallon from the eight-gallon measure	1 „	5 „	2 „
6. They fill up the three-gallon from the five-gallon measure	1 „	4 „	3 „
7. They empty the three gallons into the eight-gallon measure	4 „	4 „	0 „

Making the required equal division.

No. LXV.—The Three Market-Women. Solution.

They began by selling at the rate of three apples for a penny. The first sold ten pennyworth, the second eight pennyworth, and the third seven pennyworth. The first had then left three apples, the second five, and the third six. These they sold at one penny each, receiving, therefore, in the whole—

$$\text{The first,} \quad 10d. + 3d. = 13d.$$
$$\text{The second,} \quad 8d. + 5d. = 13d.$$
$$\text{The third,} \quad 7d. + 6d. = 13d.$$

No. LXVII.—The Farmer and his Three Daughters. Solution.

They began by selling at the rate of seven a penny, the first selling seven pennyworth, the second four, and the youngest one pennyworth. But they had saved the choicest of the fruit, the first having one apple left, the second two, and the youngest three. Meeting a liberal customer, they sold these at threepence each, and the respective amounts received by them were therefore as under—

$$\text{The first,}\quad 7d. + 3d. = 10d.$$
$$\text{The second,}\quad 4d. + 6d. = 10d.$$
$$\text{The third,}\quad 1d. + 9d. = 10d.$$

No. LXVII.—How Many for a Penny. Solution.

He bought two apples for his penny.

To arrive at the result, let x = the whole number of apples. He gives away $\dfrac{x}{3} + \dfrac{1}{3}$, and has still one apple left. Then—

$$\frac{x}{3} + \frac{1}{3} + 1 = x$$
$$\text{or } x + 1 + 3\ (= x + 4) = 3x$$
$$\therefore 2x = 4$$
$$x = 2$$

No. LXVIII —The Magic Cards. Solution.

The seven cards are drawn up on a mathematical principle, in such manner that *the first numbers of those in which a given number appears*, when added together, indicate that number.

Suppose, for instance, that the chosen number is 63. This appears in cards I., II., III., IV., V., and VI. The key numbers of these are 1, 2, 4, 8, 16, and 32; and $1 + 2 + 4 + 8 + 16 + 32 = 63$.

If the number 7 were selected, this appears only in cards I, II, and III, whose key numbers are 1, 2, and $4 = 7$.

The principle of construction seems at first sight rather mysterious, but it is simple enough when explained. The reader will note, in the first place, that the first or "key" numbers of each card form a geometrical progression, being 1, 2, 4, 8, 16, 32, 64. The total of these is 127, which is accordingly the highest number included.*

It is further to be noted that by appropriate combinations of the above figures *any* total, from 1 up to 127, can be produced.

The first card consists of the alternate numbers from 1 to 127 inclusive. The second, commencing with 2 (the second term of the geometrical series), consists of alternate groups of two consecutive figures—2, 3; 6, 7; 10, 11, and so on. The third, beginning with 4, the third term of the series, consists of alternate groups of *four* figures—4, 5, 6, 7; 12, 13, 14, 15; 20, 21, 22, 23; and so on. The fourth, commencing with 8, consists in like manner of alternate groups of *eight* figures. The fifth, commencing with 16, of alternate groups of *sixteen* figures. The sixth, commencing with 32, of alternate groups of *thirty-two* figures; and the last, commencing with 64, of a single group, being those from 64 to 127 inclusive.

It will be found that any given number of cards arranged on this principle will produce the desired result, limited by the extent of the geometrical series constituting the first numbers.

No. LXIX.—The "Fifteen" or "Boss" Puzzle. Solution.

Notwithstanding the enormous amount of energy that has been expended over the "Fifteen" Puzzle, no absolute rule for its solution has yet been discovered, and it appears to be now generally agreed by mathematicians that out of the vast number of hap-hazard positions in which the fifteen cubes may at the outset be placed,† about half admit of the blocks being so moved as to finally assume their proper order.

To test whether a given arrangement admits of such a possibility, the following rule has been suggested. Reckon how many transpositions of given pairs are necessary to

---

* If there had been six cards only, the series would have terminated with 32, and the highest number would have been 63. If eight cards were used, the final term of the series would have been 128, and its total 255, which would accordingly have been the maximum number.

† The possible number of such positions is *only* 1,307,674,368,000.

bring the blocks into the required order. If the total
number of such transpositions be even, the desired re-arrange-
ment is possible. If the number be odd, such re-arrange-
ment is impossible.

Applying this rule to the "Boss" Puzzle (see Fig. 335), it
will be seen that only *one* transposition (that of blocks 14
and 15) is here needed, and one being an *odd* number, the
problem is insoluble; as, in fact, the "Fifteen" Puzzle in
this form has been found by all who have hitherto tried it.

No. LXX.—The Peg-away Puzzle. Solution.

The possibility of success in solving this puzzle appears
to be governed by precisely the same rule as the "Fifteen"
Puzzle—viz., that if the number of needful transpositions is

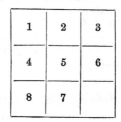

FIG. 367.   FIG. 368.

even, the puzzle can be solved; if *odd,* it is insoluble.
Thus, if the "pegs" be arranged at starting as in Fig. 367.
the aspirant will probably succeed; if as shown in Fig. 368,
he will fail.

No. LXXI.—The Over-Polite Guests. Solution.

To obtain the answer, all that is needed is to find the
number of permutations of seven objects—viz., 5040. It
would take, therefore, 5040 days, or nearly fourteen years,
to exhaust the possible positions.

In the alternative form of the problem, the host would
supply 5.040 dinners at half a crown (value £630) for a
payment of £70.

No. LXXII. – The " Royal Aquarium Thirteen." Solution.

When the puzzle is solved the arrangement of the cards will be found to be as shown in Fig. 369.

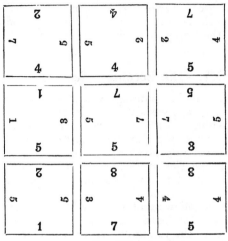

Fig. 369.

There is no royal road to the solution. The proper order must be arrived at by successive transpositions until the conditions are fulfilled.

No. LXXIII.—An Easy Creditor. Solution.

The amount of the first payment was £20.

To ascertain such amount, let x = the first payment. Then, according to the conditions of the puzzle—

$$x + \frac{x}{2} + \frac{3x}{4} + \frac{x}{4} + \frac{2x}{5} + 2 = 60$$

Multiplying by 20, the least common multiple of the various denominators,

$$20x + 10x + 15x + 5x + 8x + 40 = 1200$$
$$58x = 1200 - 40 = 1160$$
$$\therefore x = 20$$

No. LXXIV.—The Three Arabs. Solution.

The first Arab was entitled to seven, and the second to one only of the eight coins. For, the consumption being equal, each person ate $\frac{8}{3} = 2\frac{2}{3}$ loaves. Of the portion eaten by the stranger the first Arab contributed $2\frac{1}{3}$ loaves, while the second contributed $\frac{1}{3}$ loaf. The former therefore contributed seven parts, while the second contributed one only, and the proper division of the money was seven coins to the first, and one to the second.

No. LXXV.—The Eccentric Testator. Solution.

As the division left nothing over, it is clear that the share of the younger son consisted solely of the fixed sum bequeathed to him, and that there was in his case no residue on which the bequest of a ninth part could operate. Further, as the "fixed sum" gift advanced by degrees of £110, the share of such youngest son must have been £110 multiplied by the total number of inheritors. As each was to take one-ninth of a certain amount, and there was in the last case no ninth to be taken, it follows that the number of legatees was the denominator of the fraction $\frac{1}{9}$, less 1; in other words, 8.

The share of the youngest son was therefore £110 × 8 = £880; and as each of the eight took a like amount, the total value of the estate must have been £7040. Testing this sum by the conditions of the problem, the share of the eldest son is found to be

$$110 + \frac{7040 - 110}{9} = 110 + \frac{6930}{9} = 110 + 770 = 880$$

leaving a remainder of £6160.

The share of the second son will therefore be

$$220 + \frac{6160 - 220}{9} = 220 + \frac{5940}{9} = 220 + 660 = 880$$

and that of the third son

$$330 + \frac{5280 - 330}{9} = 330 + \frac{4950}{9} = 330 + 550 = 880$$

and so on throughout, the increasing value of the fixed amount exactly compensating for the diminished value of the fraction.

No. LXXVI.—Another Eccentric Testator. Solution.

The estate amounted to the sum of £7200, and each son took an equal share—*i.e.*, £1440.

For convenience of reference, we will call what remained after the eldest son had taken his share the *first* residue; what remained after the second had taken his share, the *second* residue; what remained after the third had taken his share, the *third* residue; and what remained after the fourth had taken his share, the *fourth* residue.

Now, according to the conditions of the problem, the fifth son took one half of the fourth residue, *plus* £720. As the fourth residue was thereby exhausted, with no remainder, it is clear that the £720 constituted the remaining half of such residue, and that the fourth residue therefore consisted of twice £720, or £1440.

The fourth son took $\frac{1}{3}$ of the third residue, *plus* £480, and what remained after these two deductions constituted the fourth residue, whose value we have found to be £1440. In other words, $\frac{2}{3}$ of the third residue, *less* £480 = £1440, and $\frac{2}{3}$ of the third residue = £1440 + £480, or £1920. Two-thirds of the third residue being £1920, the whole, or $\frac{3}{3}$, of such residue, must be £2880.

As the third son took $\frac{1}{4}$ of the second residue, *plus* £360, and there then remained £2880, $\frac{3}{4}$ of the second residue must in like manner = £2880 + £360, or £3240, and the whole of such second residue must be £3240 + £1080 = £4320.

As the second son took $\frac{1}{5}$ of the first residue, *plus* £288, and there was then left £4320, we deduce, by a like process of reasoning, that the amount of the first residue was £5760.

As the eldest son took $\frac{1}{6}$ of the whole property, *plus* £240, and there was then left £5760, it is clear, in like manner, that $\frac{5}{6}$ of the whole inheritance was £5760 + 240, or £6000; and if £6000 represent $\frac{5}{6}$, the whole will necessarily be £7,200.

Testing the correctness of our demonstration by the conditions of the puzzle, we find that—

The eldest son takes $\frac{7200}{6} + 240 = 1200 + 240 =$ £1440.

First residue $7200 - 1440 = 5760$.

The second son takes $\frac{5760}{5} + 288 = 1152 + 288 = 1440$.

Second residue 5760 — 1440 = 4320.

The third son takes $\dfrac{4320}{4}$ + 360 = 1080 + 360 = 1440.

Third residue 4320 — 1440 = 2880.

The fourth son takes $\dfrac{2880}{3}$ + 480 = 960 + 480 = 1440.

Fourth residue 2880 — 1440 = 1440.

The fifth son takes $\dfrac{1440}{2}$ + 720 = 720 + 720 = 1400.

Total £7200.

No. LXXVII.—An Aggravating Uncle. Solution.

The number of soldiers was 58.

On examination of the conditions of the puzzle, it will be found that in each case, whether divided by 3, 4, 5, or 6, there are always *two* short of an even division. All that is needed, therefore, is to find the least common multiple of 3, 4, 5, and 6, and deduct 2 from it. The L.C.M. of 3, 4, 5, and 6 is 60, and 60 − 2 = 58, the required number.

No. LXXVIII.—The Apples and Oranges. Solution.

As each child had 3 more oranges than apples, and this caused a difference of 33 (48 − 15) in the number left over, it follows that the number of children must have been 11. As each child received 12 apples, and there were 48 over, the total number of apples must have been (11 × 12) + 48 = 132 + 48 = 180. As each child received 15 oranges, and there were 15 over, the total number of oranges must have been (11 × 15) + 15 = 165 + 15 = 180.

No. LXXIX.—The Two Squares. Solution.

As the 146 counters remaining from the first arrangement were insufficient by 31 to make the two additional rows desired, the actual number needed for such two rows must have been 146 + 31 = 177. Of these, one (the counter at the corner) would be common to both rows, and the number in one row would therefore be $\frac{176}{2} + 1 = 89$.

A square of 89 counters each way would be $89 \times 89 = 7921$. But according to the terms of the problem the actual number of counters was 31 short of this—*i.e.*, 7890.

The correctness of this conclusion may be tested by calculating the number in the original square, which was one counter less (viz., 88) each way. The square of 88 is 7744. But in this case there were 146 counters left over. $7744 + 146 = 7890$, the same number arrived at by the first process.

No. LXXX.—A Curious Division. Solution.

To ascertain the common quotient, add together the three divisors, 3, 6, and 9, and divide 7890 by their total, 18. The quotient is $438\frac{1}{3}$. Multiply the number thus obtained by 3, 6, and 9 respectively, and the three products will give the numbers contained in the three heaps.

Thus—
$$438\frac{1}{3} \times 3 = 1315$$
$$438\frac{1}{3} \times 6 = 2630$$
$$438\frac{1}{3} \times 9 = 3945$$

$$\overline{7890}$$

No. LXXXI.—A Curious Multiplication. Solution.

This is a very much easier problem, as the proportions of the four heaps are almost self-evident. Taking the fourth, or smallest heap, as the unit of measurement, and calling it 1 accordingly, the third, which is of obviously double the size (as requiring to be multiplied by 6 only, instead of 12, to raise it to the same amount), will $= 2$. The second heap will in like manner $= 3$, and the first $= 4$, and their collective values will be $1 + 2 + 3 + 4 = 10$. Divide the whole number by this amount; the quotient is 789. This gives us the value of our unit of measurement, and from it we may deduce the value of all four heaps, thus :—

The fourth heap contains		789 counters.
The third „ „	$789 \times 2 =$	1578 „
The second „ „	$789 \times 3 =$	2367 „
The first „ „	$789 \times 4 =$	3156 „
	Total	7890	

No. LXXXII.—The Two Schoolmasters. Solution.

The difference was 6, the smaller school having 66 pupils only.

For, inasmuch as one-sixth of the pupils were away ill, the remainder, viz.—

11 haymaking,

7 at the fair,

and 37 at school,

together making 55—must have been five-sixths of the whole number, and $55 \div 5 (= 11)$, one-sixth. The whole number of the smaller school was therefore $11 \times 6 = 66$.

No. LXXXIII.—Nothing Left. Solution.

The required number is 118.

To obtain it, work the process indicated in reverse order, as follows :—

$$
\begin{aligned}
0 + 18 &= 18 \\
18^2 &= 324 \\
324 \div 3 &= 108 \\
108 + 10 &= 118
\end{aligned}
$$

No. LXXXIV.—The Three Generations. Solution.

The old man was 69, his son 40, and his grandson 16.

As the old man and his son were together 109 years old, and the old man and his grandson only 85 years old, it follows that the age of the son was $109-85 (=24)$ years greater than that of the grandson. As the son and grandson were together 56 years old, and the former was 24 years older than the latter, it follows that the grandson's age was

$$\frac{56-24}{2} = \frac{32}{2} = 16 \text{ years.}$$

The son's age was therefore $16 + 24 = 40$ years.

As the united ages of the old man and his son were together 109, the age of the former must have been $109-40 = 69$ years.

No. LXXXV.—The Two Brothers. Solution.

As $\frac{2}{3}$ of the age of the younger is $\frac{5}{12}$ that of the elder, the actual age of the younger must be $\dfrac{5 + 2\frac{1}{2}}{12} = \dfrac{7\frac{1}{2}}{12} = \dfrac{15}{24} = \dfrac{5}{8}$

that of the elder, and the difference between them $\frac{3}{8}$ that of the elder. By the terms of the question, we know that this $\frac{3}{8} = 9$ years, in which case $\frac{1}{8}$ must $= 3$ years, and the whole age of the elder $3 \times 8 (= 24)$ years. The age of the younger will consequently be $24 - 9 = 15$ years.

No. LXXXVI.—The Two Sons. Solution.

The younger son is $24\frac{1}{2}$; the elder, $29\frac{3}{4}$ years old.

The solution is most easily got at by means of a simple equation, thus :—

Let y = age of younger.

Then $y + 5\frac{1}{4}$ = age of elder.

By the terms of the question —

$$5y + 6(y + 5\frac{1}{4}) = 301$$
$$5y + 6y + 31\frac{1}{2} = 301$$
$$11y = 301 - 31\frac{1}{2} = 269\frac{1}{2}$$
$$y = 24\frac{1}{2}$$

The younger son is therefore $24\frac{1}{2}$ years old, and the elder $24\frac{1}{2} + 5\frac{1}{4} = 29\frac{3}{4}$.

No. LXXXVII.—The Two Nephews. Solution.

The one was 18, the other 6 years old.

It is clear that as the larger number is three times the smaller, it must be a multiple of 3. It cannot be a larger number than 18, because the square of the next multiple of 3—viz., 21—would alone exceed 360. We proceed to try 18 accordingly as the larger number, and $\frac{18}{3}$ (=6) as the smaller number, when we find that $18^2 + 6^2 = 324 + 36 = 360$, the total required. 18 and 6 years are therefore the respective ages.

No. LXXXVIII.—The Reversed Number.   Solution.

The required number is 45. It may be got at either algebraically or arithmetically. In the first case—

Let x = the first, or left-hand, digit,

and y = the second, or right-hand, digit.

Then (as x represents *tens*) $10x + y$ will be the total number, and $10y + x$ the number produced by reversing its digits, while $x + y$ will be the sum of such digits. Now, by the terms of the question,

$$10x + y = 5(x + y)$$
$$= 5x + 5y$$
$$\therefore 5x = 4y$$
$$\text{And } x = \frac{4y}{5}$$

Further, by the terms of the question—

$$10x + y + 9 = 10y + x.$$

Substituting the value above obtained for x—

we have $$\frac{40y}{5} + y + 9 = 10y + \frac{4y}{5}$$
or, $$40y + 5y + 45 = 50y + 4y$$
$$45y + 45 = 54y$$
$$9y = 45$$
$$y = 5$$

Then $$x \left(= \frac{4y}{5} \right) = 4$$

and $10x + y$ (the whole number) = 45.

The arithmetical process is, however, in this case the simpler, thus—

As the required number is equal to five times the sum of its digits (*i.e.*, a multiple of 5), its final digit must be 5 or 0*. But such final digit is also the first digit of the reversed number.   0 would not answer this condition, and the final digit must therefore be 5.   Nine added to any number ending in 5 makes the final digit 4.   This gives us the reversed number as 54, and the actual number consequently as 45, which is found to fully answer the required conditions.

* See *Properties of Numbers*, p. 177.

No. LXXXIX.—Another Reversed Number.
Solution.

The required number is 42.

Here again either the algebraical method or the arithmetical method may be used. Let $x =$ the first digit, and y the second digit. Then $10x + y =$ the required number, and $10y + x =$ the reversed number.

By the terms of the problem—

$$(1) \qquad 10x + y = 7(x + y)$$
$$(2) \quad 10x + y - 18 = 10y + a$$
$$10x + y = 7x + 7y$$
$$3x = 6y$$
$$x = 2y$$

Substituting this value in equation (2), we have

$$20y + y - 18 = 10y + 2y$$
$$21y - 18 = 12y$$
$$9y = 18$$
$$y = 2$$

and as $x = 2y$ the number must be 42.

The arithmetical or logical process is as follows :—

By the terms of the question, the required number is a multiple of 7. As it has only two digits, and its remainder *less* 18 is also a number of two digits, this limits the selection to 35, 42, 49, 56, 63, 72, 77, 84, 91, or 98. Among these the only number which answers the remaining conditions is 42, which is accordingly the answer.

No. XC.—The Shepherd and his Sheep. Solution.

There were in the first fold				27
,,	,,	,,	second	25
,,	,,	,,	third	18
,,	,,	,,	fourth	16
,,	,,	,,	fifth	14
			Total	100

For as there were—

In the first and second folds	52
„ second and third	43
„ third and fourth	34
„ fourth and fifth	30

The number in the first and fifth, with double the respective numbers in the second, third and fourth, will be   159

As the actual number is 100, it follows that the number in the second, third and fourth folds = 159 − 100 = 59.

And as there were in the second and third 43, the number in the fourth fold must have been 59 − 43 = 16.

As there were in the fourth and fifth 30, the number in the fifth fold must have been 30 − 16 = 14.

As in the third and fourth there were 34, the number in the third fold must have been 34 − 16 = 18.

In like manner, the number in the second fold was 43 − 18 = 25.

And the number in the first fold was 52 − 25 = 27.

$$27 + 25 + 18 + 16 + 14 = 100.$$

No. XCI.—The Shepherdess and her Sheep. Solution.

The numbers are 7, 14, 28, and 56 respectively.

By the terms of the question, it appears that the numbers in the four folds are in geometrical progression, with a common ratio of 2. Taking experimentally the smallest possible such progression, we find it to be $1 + 2 + 4 = 8 = 15$. But the total of the actual progression is stated to be 105. Dividing this by 15, we have as quotient 7, which we use as a common multiplier to bring the series up to the required total. Thus:—

$$7 \times 1 = 7$$
$$7 \times 2 = 14$$
$$7 \times 4 = 28$$
$$7 \times 8 = 56$$

Total   105

No. XCII.—A Weighty Matter. Solution.

Seven weights are required, of 1, 2, 4, 8, 16, 32, and 64 lbs. respectively, together making 127 lbs. It will be found that, by using one, two, or more of these, any weight from 1 to 127 lbs. can be weighed.*

No. XCIII.—The Three Topers. Solution.

The quantity would be consumed in $4\frac{16}{31}$ hours.

For—as Peter can drink 40 quarts in 20 hours, he would drink in 1 hour $\frac{40}{20}=2$ quarts.

As Paul can drink 40 quarts in 14 hours, he would drink in 1 hour $\frac{40}{14}=2\frac{6}{7}$ quarts.

As Roger can drink 40 quarts in 10 hours: he would drink in 1 hour $\frac{40}{10}=4$ quarts.

And they would together drink in 1 hour $2 + 2\frac{6}{7} + 4$ (= $8\frac{6}{7}$) quarts, and 40 quarts in $(40 \div 8\frac{6}{7}) = 4\frac{16}{31}$ hours.

No. XCIV.—The False Scales. Solution.

Answer, 12 lbs.

Problems of this class are solved by ascertaining the square root of the product of the two weights.

In this case $9 \times 16 = 144$, and $\sqrt{144} = 12$, the required answer.

No. XCV.—An Arithmetical Policeman. Solution.

The hour struck was twelve.

The fractions mentioned, $\frac{1}{2}$, $\frac{1}{3}$, and $\frac{1}{4}$, if regarded as fractions of a single hour, will be found, when added together, to amount to $1\frac{1}{12}$ of an hour. To raise the surplus $\frac{1}{12}$ to the value of a complete hour, it must be multiplied by 12, and 12 is therefore the hour that was struck.

---

* The numbers, it will be observed, are in geometrical progression. For another illustration of the fact here stated, see The Magic Cards, p. 161.

No. XCVI.—The Flock of Geese. Solution.

The number of the flock was 36.

For, taking the lowest number (4), which is divisible by 2 and by 4 (as, from the conditions of the problem, it is clear that the required number must be), and going through the process suggested with such number, we have the following result:—

4 + 4 (as many more) + 2 (half as many more) + 1 (one-fourth as many more) = 11.

Dividing 99 (the total to be obtained after going through the same process with the actual number in the flock) by the number thus obtained, we find the quotient to be 9. 4, therefore, multiplied by 9 (= 36) should be the required number. Putting it to the test, we find that 36 + 36 + 18 + 9 = 99, exactly answering the conditions.

No. XCVII.—The Divided Cord. Solution.

The one portion is 16, and the other 20 inches.

As the one segment is to be $\frac{4}{5}$ of the other, their respective proportions will be 4 to 5, or in all 9 parts. One ninth part of 36 inches is 4 inches. Taking this as the unit of measurement, we find that—

$$\text{the longer segment is } 5'' \times 4'' = 20 \text{ inches,}$$
$$\text{and the shorter } \quad \text{,,} \quad \text{,,} \quad 4'' \times 4'' = 16 \quad \text{,,}$$
$$\text{Together, } \quad \underline{\underline{36}} \quad \text{,,}$$

No. XCVIII.—The Divided Number. Solution.

The parts are 28 and 18 respectively.

It is clear from the conditions of the problem that the first part is a multiple of 7, and the second a multiple of 3. Now there are in the number 46 six multiples of 7—viz., 7, 14, 21, 28, 35, and 42. In like manner there are in the same number fifteen multiples of 3—viz., 3, 6, 9, 12, 15, 18, 21, 24, 27, 30, 33, 36, 39, 42, and 45. Of these, the only pairs which together make 46 are 7 and 39, and 28 and 18. The first pair clearly does not answer the conditions of the

question, for $\frac{7}{7} + \frac{39}{3} = 1 + 13 = 14$. We proceed to try the
second pair, and find that $\frac{28}{7} + \frac{18}{3} = 4 + 6 = 10$. 28 and 18
are therefore the required numbers.

By the aid of algebra the problem may be solved much
more neatly. Thus—
Let $x =$ the portion to be divided by 7, and y the portion
to be divided by 3.
Then, by the terms of the question—

$$x + y = 46$$
$$i.e. \quad x = 46 - y.$$

Further, $\quad \dfrac{x}{7} + \dfrac{y}{3} = 10$

or, substituting the value above found for x—

$$\frac{46 - y}{7} + \frac{y}{3} = 10$$
$$3 (46 - y) + 7y = 210$$
$$138 - 3y + 7y = 210$$
$$4y = 210 - 138 = 72$$
$$y = 18$$

And as $x = 46 - y$
$$x = 46 - 18$$
$$= 28.$$

No. XCIX.—The Two Numbers.   Solution.

The required numbers are 5 and 7.   For if twice the
first + the second = 17, and twice the second + the first =
19, then the above added together—*i.e.*, three times the first
+ three times the second must be 17 + 19 = 36, and the
sum of the numbers themselves must be $\frac{36}{3} = 12$.

And since twice the first + the second is an odd number,
the second is also an odd number, and the first, being an
even number (12) *less* an odd number, must also be an odd
number.[*]

---

[*] Because twice any whole number is always an even number; and
an even number *plus* an even number is always an even number.   See
p. 174.

Now the only pairs of odd numbers which together make 12 are 1 and 11, 3 and 9, and 5 and 7. Of these, we find by experiment that 5 and 7 are the only two that answer the conditions; $5 \times 2 + 7 = 17$, and $7 \times 2 + 5 = 19$.

Here again the problem is much more readily solved by algebra. Thus—

$$\text{Let } x = \text{first number,}$$
$$\text{And } y = \text{second number.}$$

We have then the equations

$$2x + y = 17$$
$$2y + x = 19$$

From the latter equation we deduce that

$$x = 19 - 2y.$$

Substituting this value in the first equation, we get

$$2(19 - 2y) + y = 17$$
$$38 - 4y + y = 17$$
$$or \qquad 3y = 38 - 17 = 21$$
$$y = 7.$$

Substituting this value in the second equation—

$$2y + x = 19$$
$$\text{we have } 14 + x = 19$$
$$x = 19 - 14$$
$$= 5$$

No. C.—The Horse and Trap.   Solution.

The horse cost £60, and the trap £25.

As five times the value of the horse=twelve times the value of the trap, it is clear that the latter was worth $\frac{5}{12}$ as much as the former. The value of the two together may, therefore, be expressed as $1 + \frac{5}{12}$ (or $\frac{17}{12}$), and this by the conditions of the problem=£85. If $\frac{17}{12}$ of the value of the horse be £85, $\frac{1}{12}$ of such value will be $\frac{1}{17}$ of that amount— *i.e.*, £5. The total value of the horse is therefore £5 × 12= £60. The value of the trap, being $\frac{5}{12}$ of £60, is £25.

No. CI.—The Two Workmen. Solution.

They must work $6\frac{2}{9}$ hours per day.

For A, doing the whole in 70 hours, does $\frac{1}{70}$ in 1 hour.

And B, doing the whole in 56 hours, does $\frac{1}{56}$ in 1 hour.

Or, together, in 1 hour $\frac{1}{70} + \frac{1}{56} = \frac{4}{280} + \frac{5}{280} = \frac{9}{280}$.

They would, therefore, do the whole in $\frac{280}{9} = 31\frac{1}{9}$ hours.

And to complete it in 5 days, they must work $\dfrac{31\frac{1}{9}}{5} = 6\frac{2}{9}$

hours per day.

No. CII.—The Divided Number. Solution.

The required numbers are 120, 72, and 45.

For since 3 times the first = 5 times the second, the second must be $\frac{3}{5}$ of the first.

And since 3 times the first = 8 times the third, the third must be $\frac{3}{8}$ of the first.

The three parts are therefore as 1, $\frac{3}{5}$, and $\frac{3}{8}$, or as 40, 24, and 15.

Now, $40 + 24 + 15 = 79$, and $237 \div 79 = 3$.

Using this as a common multiplier, we have

$$\therefore \quad \begin{array}{rcl} 40 \times 3 &=& 120 = \text{first part.} \\ 24 \times 3 &=& 72 = \text{second part.} \\ 15 \times 3 &=& 45 = \text{third part.} \\ \hline & & 237 \end{array}$$

No. CIII.—The Three Reapers. Solution.

As A, B, and C, working simultaneously, reap the field in 5 days, it is obvious that they together reap in one day $\frac{1}{5}$ of it. Now A's and C's day's work are together equal to twice B's. Therefore B's *plus* twice B's (or three times B's) also $= \frac{1}{5}$; and B's day's work = one-third of $\frac{1}{5} = \frac{1}{15}$.

Further, as A's and B's day's work together = three times C's, then C's plus three times C's (= four times C's) also = $\frac{1}{5}$, and C's day's work = $\frac{1}{4}$ of $\frac{1}{5} = \frac{1}{20}$.

Again, as all three together in one day do $\frac{1}{5}$, A must in one day do $\frac{1}{5} - \left(\frac{1}{15} + \frac{1}{20}\right)$.

$$= \frac{12 - (4+3)}{60} = \frac{12-7}{60} = \frac{5}{60} = \frac{1}{12}.$$

A would therefore take 12 days, *B* 15 days, and *C* 20 days to do the work singly.

No. CIV.—The Bag of Marbles. Solution.

If when Tom takes 4, Jack takes 3, and if when Tom takes 6, Dick takes 7, then when Tom takes 12 (the least common multiple of 4 and 6), Jack and Dick will take 9 and 14 respectively, and they will together have taken 12 + 9 + 14 = 35 marbles. Now 35 is contained in 770 22 times, and therefore :—

Tom's share will be $12 \times 22 = 264$
Jack's   „ $9 \times 22 = 198$
Dick's   „ $14 \times 22 = 308$
                              $\overline{770}$

Again, their respective ages will be as 12, 9, and 14 ; but 12, 9, and 14 together make 35, and the total of their ages is only $17\frac{1}{2}$ years, or one-half of 35. Their ages are therefore one-half the above figures, or 6, $4\frac{1}{2}$, and 7 respectively.

No. CV.—The Expunged Numerals. A. Solution.

The puzzle is solved by striking out the first figure of the top row, the whole of the second row, and the two first figures of the last row. The sum will then stand as under :—

$$\begin{array}{r} .\,11 \\ \cdot\ \cdot\ \cdot \\ .\,.\,9 \\ \hline 20 \end{array}$$

No. CVI.—The Expunged Numerals. B. Solution.

The dots indicate the figures to be expunged.

$$\begin{array}{r} .\,11 \\ 33\,. \\ \cdot\ \cdot\ \cdot \\ 77\,. \\ \cdot\ \cdot\ \cdot \\ \hline 1111 \end{array}$$

No. CVII.—A Tradesman in a Difficulty. Solution.

1. The purchaser gives his one-dollar and his two-cent piece to the tradesman, and his three-cent piece to the stranger.

2. The tradesman gives his half-dollar to the purchaser, and his quarter-dollar to the stranger.

3. The stranger gives his two dimes and his one-cent piece to the purchaser, and his five-cent piece and his two-cent piece to the tradesman, when each has his right amount.

The correctness of the arrangement is not at once obvious, but it is easily proved. For the sake of brevity, we will call the purchaser P, the tradesman T, and the stranger S.

P has at the outset 1 dollar, 3 cents, and 2 cents, together = 105 cents. He should, therefore, have left, after paying for his goods, $105 - 34 = 71$ cents.

T has at the outset a half-dollar and a quarter-dollar, together = 75 cents. After receiving payment for his goods he should, therefore, have $75 + 34 = 109$ cents.

S has 2 dimes, 5 cents, 2 cents, and 1 cent, in all 28 cents. He has neither to gain nor lose by the transaction, so should be left at the close with the same amount. Let us now see how these figures correspond with the result of the transaction.

P parts with 1 dollar and 2 cents to T, and 3 cents to S, in all 105 cents. He has therefore no cash of his own left; but he receives from T 50 cents and from S 21 cents. He has, therefore, at the close of the transaction $50 + 21 = 71$ cents. T hands to P half a dollar, and to S a quarter-dollar; but, on the other hand, he receives from P 1 dollar and 2 cents, and from S 7 cents—in all, 109 cents.

S has given 2 dimes and 1 cent to P, and 7 cents to the tradesman. This (= 28 cents in all) clears him out. On the other hand, he receives from S a quarter-dollar, and from P 3 cents, which also together amount to 28 cents.

Each has therefore received the precise amount to which he was entitled.

No. CVIII.—Profit and Loss. Solution.

The original cost was £2 18*s*. 3*d*.

The difference between the marked price (65 shillings) and

the price obtained (56 shillings) is 9 shillings. This sum represents the amount of the actual loss, *plus* three times the amount of such loss (which latter item would have been the profit)—in all, four times the amount of the loss. The loss was, therefore, $\frac{9}{4}$ shillings, or 2s. 3d. Add this amount to the price obtained, £2 16s., and we have £2 18s. 3d., the cost price.

No. CIX.—A Curious Fraction. Solution.

The fraction in question is $\frac{240}{253}$.

To obtain the result, take the three denominations named, £1, 1s., and 1d : reduce all to pence, and add them together. The total $(240 + 12 + 1 = 253)$ will give us the denominator of the required fraction, while the value of £1 in pence (240) will be the numerator. The process is perhaps clearer in algebra. Thus :—

Let $\frac{x}{y}$ be the required fraction.

Then $\frac{x}{y}$ pounds $+ \frac{x}{y}$ shillings $+ \frac{x}{y}$ pence $= 1$ pound.

Or, reducing all to the " pence " denomination—

$$\frac{240x + 12x + x}{y} = 240$$

$$\frac{253x}{y} = 240$$

$$\frac{x}{y} = \frac{240}{253}$$

Examining the correctness of the above result, we find that

$\frac{240}{253}$ of £1 $= 18s. 11\frac{169}{253}d.$

$\frac{240}{253}$ of 1s. $= 11\frac{97}{253}d.$

$\frac{240}{253}$ of 1d. $= \frac{240}{253}d.$

_____

£1   0   0

No. CX.—The Menagerie. Solution.

There being 36 heads (*i.e.*, 36 creatures in all), if all had been birds they would have had 72 feet. If all had been beasts, they would have had 144 feet. It is clear, therefore, that there were some of each. Suppose the numbers equal, the feet would then count as under:—

18 birds : 36 feet.
18 beasts : 72 feet.

$\overline{36}$ $\overline{108}$ feet (being an excess of 8 over the stated number.)

Each bird added to the "bird" half (involving at the same time the deduction therefrom of one beast) produces a diminution of 2 in the number of feet. As the equal division gives an excess of 8 feet, we must therefore deduct 4 beasts and add 4 birds.

This gives us $18+4=22$ birds, having 44 feet.
$18-4=14$ beasts   ,,   56   ,,

$\overline{36}$ $\overline{100}$

No. CXI.—The Market Woman and her Eggs. Solution.

Her original stock was seven.

To discover it, it is sufficient to note that she gave her last customer half her remaining stock, *plus* half an egg. As this left her with none, the half egg must have been equal to the half of her then stock, which must, therefore, have been 1 egg only. She gave the second customer *half* her then stock, *plus* half an egg; and as this left her with one egg only, it is obvious that the half in question must have been $1\frac{1}{2}$ egg. She had, therefore, prior to this second transaction 3 eggs left. At the first sale she gave half her original stock, *plus* half an egg, and as this left her with 3 eggs, it follows that her original stock must have been 7.

No CXII.—The Cook and his Assistants. Solution.

His original stock was 39. He gave half *plus* half an egg (*i.e.*, 20) to the first assistant. This left him with 19. He gave half of these *plus* half an egg ($9\frac{1}{2}+\frac{1}{2}=10$) to the second assistant, and had then 9 left. He gave half of these *plus* half an egg ($4\frac{1}{2}+\frac{1}{2}=5$) to the third assistant, and had 4 left.

The method of obtaining the solution is the same as in the last case.

The reader may be interested to know how problems of this class are constructed. As the division is by moieties, 2 is taken as the basis number, and this is raised to the power corresponding to the number of divisions. Thus in the two cases supposed, of *three* divisions, we take $2^3 = 8$. Multiply this by any number you please ; subtract 1 from the result. The ultimate remainder, when the original number has been three times diminished as described, will be less by 1 than the number you multiplied by. Thus if we take as the starting-point,—

$(8 \times 1) - 1 = 7$, the ultimate remainder will be *nil*.
$(8 \times 2) - 1 = 15$,   „   „   „   1.
$(8 \times 3) - 1 = 23$,   „   „   „   2.
$(8 \times 4) - 1 = 31$,   „   „   „   3.
$(8 \times 5) - 1 = 39$,   „   „   „   4.
and so on.

Why the process indicated should have this peculiar result is a further puzzle, which we will leave to the ingenuity of our mathematical readers.

CHAPTER II.

No. I.—A Puzzling Inscription.

The following queer inscription is said to be found in the chancel of a small church in Wales, just over the Ten Commandments. The addition of a single letter, repeated at various intervals, renders it not only intelligible, but appropriate to the situation:

P R S V R Y P R F C T M N

V R K P T H S P R C P T S T N.

What is the missing letter?

No. II.—An Easy One.

E D O R N O W.

Make one word of the above letters.

No. III.—Pied Proverbs.

Each of the following series of letters, duly arranged, will be found to form a popular proverb.

A. aeegghillmnnnoooorrsssstt.

B. aaceeeffhhiiiiimnoooprrssttttt.

C. aaaddeefiiimmnnnnoorttw.

D. aabbddeehhhhhiiiinnnoorrssttttuww.

95

E. aadegghiilllllnoorssttttt.

F. abdeefiinnnoopprrrsssttuw.

G. aabdeeeeefffhiiikmnnnrrsst.

H. aadeeehllllllnssttww.

No. IV.—Scattered Sentiment.

Daruno em hslal verho,
Ni dasesns ro lege,
Lilt silfe rdaems eb vero,
Twees riemem's fo ethe.

The above, duly re-arranged, will be found to form a couplet suitable for a valentine.

No. V.—Dropped-Letter Proverbs.

Supply the missing letters, and each of the series following will be found to represent a popular proverb.*

a. A-t-t-h-n-t-m-s-v-s-n-n.

b. F-i-t-h-a-t-e-e-w-n-a-r-a-y.

c. S-r-k-w-i-e-h-i-o-s-h-t.

d. H-l-g-s-b-s-w-o-a-g-s-l-t.

e. B-r-s-f-f-t-r-f-c-t-g-t-r.

f. H-w-o-g-s-b-r-w-g-g-s-s-r-w-g.

g. C-l-r-n-d-f-o-s-p-k-h-t-t-h.

h. W-e-t-e-w-n-s-n-h-w-t-s-t.

---

* Each dash represents either a dropped letter or the space between two words. In some of the later examples one dash stands for two dropped letters.

i. S-r-r-k-n-n-s-m-k-l-n-f-n-s.

k. H-n-s-y-s-t-b-s-p-l-c-.

l. A-p-n-d-y-s-g-t-y-r.

m. T-k-c-r-f-h-p-n-n-t-e-p-n-s-w-l-t-k-c-r-f-t-e-s-l-s.

No. VI.—Dropped-Letter Nursery Rhymes.

The following, the missing letters being duly supplied, will be found to represent familar quotations of the juvenile order :—

(1.) H-w-o-h-h-l-t-l-b-s-b-e
   I-p-o-e-a-h-h-n-n-h-u-;
   H-g-t-e-s-o-e-a-l-h-d-y
   F-o-e-e-y-p-n-n-f-o-e-.

(2.) J-c-a-d-i-l-e-t-p-h-h-l-
   T-f-t-h-p-i-o-w-t-r :
   J-c-f-l-d-w-a-d-r-k-h-s-r-w-
   A-d-i-l-a-e-u-b-i-g-f-e-.

(3.) H-y-i-d-e-i-d-e-h-c-t-n-t-e-i-d-l-
   T-e-o-j-m-e-o-e-t-e-o-n
   T-e-i-t-e-o-l-u-h-d-o-e-s-c-f-n-s-o-t
   A-d-h-d-s-r-n-w-y-i-h-h-s-o-n.

No. VII.—Transformations.

This is a form of word-puzzle that deserves to be better known, as it may be made productive of considerable amuse-ment. It consists in taking a word of a given number of letters, and trying in how many "moves" or transpositions, altering only one letter each time, you can transform it into some other pre-arranged word of the like number of letters, but of different or opposite meaning ; as Light into Heavy, Rose into Lily, Hard into Easy, or the like. Each step of the process must be a known word. We will take the last-named pair as an example. Five "moves" will in this case suffice, as under :—

Hard—(1) card, (2) cart, (3) cast, (4), east, (5) Easy.

This, however, is a more than usually favourable specimen, one of the letters, *a*, being common to both words, and, therefore, requiring no change. A considerably larger number of moves will usually be found necessary.*

The reader is invited to transform :—

> Hand into Foot—in six moves.
> Sin into Woe—in three moves.
> Hate into Love—in three moves.
> Black into White—in eight moves.
> Wood into Coal—in three moves.
> Blue into Pink—in four moves.
> Cat into Dog—in three moves.
> More into Less—in four moves.
> Rose into Lily—in five moves.
> Shoe into Boot—in three moves.†

No. VIII.—Beheaded Words.

1. Behead a tree, and leave the roof of a vault.
2. Behead "on high," and leave the topmost story.
3. Behead "thrown violently," and leave an organ of the body.
4. Behead a preposition, and leave a contest.
5. Behead your own property, and leave ours.
6. Behead to delete, and leave to destroy.
7. Behead a reproach, and leave a relative.
8. Behead to annoy, and leave comfort.
9. Behead an occurrence, and leave an airhole.

The deleted initials, taken in the above order, will give the name of an American general, after whom a well-known street in Paris is named.

---

* Unless one or more letters are common to both words, the number of moves cannot possibly be *less* than the number of letters in each word.

† Where several persons take part, this may be made a very amusing game. Certain pairs of words having been agreed upon, each takes the list, and tries in how few moves he can effect the required transformations, the player with the smallest total winning the game.

No. IX.—Anagrams.

An anagram is defined by Ogilvie as "the transposition of the letters of a name, by which a new word is formed." This definition hardly goes far enough, inasmuch as it ignores the far more interesting class of anagrams, in which the letters of a whole sentence are re-arranged so as to assume a different sense. To be worthy of serious consideration, however, the anagram must have a further quality—viz., that the new rendering must have some sort of relation to the original. In some cases a new rendering of this kind has happened to be singularly appropriate; so much so, indeed, that in less enlightened times people have claimed for anagrams a sort of inspiration, or magical significance. There is a historic instance in the case of James I., of England, whose name, *James Stuart*, was transposed by his courtiers, to his great delight, into *A just master*, and who was more than half persuaded of his descent from the mythical King Arthur, on the ground that his full name, *Charles James Stuart*, was capable of transposition into *Claims Arthur's Seat.* Another well-known instance is that of Lady Eleanor Davies, wife of the poet, Sir John Davies (*temp.*, Charles I.), who claimed to be a prophetess, on the somewhat unsubstantial ground that the letters of her name, *Dame Eleanor Davies*, duly shuffled, form the sentence *Reveal, O Daniel.* Her pretensions ultimately caused her to be arraigned before the Court of High Commission, when the Dean of Arches pointed out that the same letters might also read *Never so mad a ladie.* The public preferred the latter rendering, and no more was heard of the *soi-disant* prophetess.

A recent prize competition among readers of *Tit-Bits*, for the best anagrammatic rendering of the title of either of the articles in a given number, produced the following, "Dangers of amateur physicking," "The sick men pay for drugs again." This is a model of what an anagram should be, and we can well understand a credulous person believing that there must be something more than mere chance in so pregnant a warning.

The following are instances of specially meritorious anagrams, in various languages :—

Ie charme tout, an anagrammatic rendering, attributed to

Henri IV., of the name of *Marie Touchet*, the mistress of Charles IX.

Honor est a Nilo—Horatio Nelson.

Quid est veritas? (the Latin rendering of Pilate's question, " What is truth ? "). *Est vir qui adest*—" It is the man who is before you."

Flit on, cheering angel.—Florence Nightingale.

The Tichborne trial gave rise to a somewhat complicated anagram. *Sir Roger Charles Doughty Tichborne, Baronet—You horrid butcher, Orton, biggest rascal here.*

We append a brief selection for our readers to exercise their ingenuity upon.

a. Rare mad frolic.   Transposed, represents—a political cry.

b. Got a scant religion :—the name of a prominent division of Nonconformists.

c. Best in prayer :—ditto, ditto.

d. Lady mine :—what every unmarried lady should be.

e. City life :—happiness.

f. Tournament :—a description of tilting.

g. Melodrama :—what melodrama ought to be.

h. Misanthrope :—what he deserves.

i. Old England :—the same country poetically described.

j. Telegraphs :—what they are to commerce.

k. Lawyers :—a satirical description of themselves.

l. Astronomers :—ditto.

m. Astronomers :—their occupation gone.

No. X.—Word Squares.

The problem in this case is to arrange a series of words, having the like number of letters each, one above the other, in such manner that they shall read alike, whether in a horizontal or vertical direction. The following are examples of sixteen letter squares.

Take the equivalent (a word in four letters) of—

a.

1. A narrow road.
2. A plane surface.
3. A preposition signifying propinquity.
4. Two parts of the body.

b.

1. Not any.
2. Across.
3. Not far.
4. Does wrong.

c.

1. Halting.
2. Dry.
3. A possessive pronoun.
4. Paradise.

d.

1. A burden.
2. A river.
3. Begs.
4. A piece of writing-furniture.

e.

1. A puppet.
2. A river.
3. A wild beast.
4. Solitary.

f.

1. A noted city.
2. A stone, reputed unlucky.
3. To knock about.
4. A girl's name.

The next two examples are of words of *five* and *six* letters :—

g.

1. To squander.
2. A stage player.
3. A mineral concretion.
4. A pick-me-up.
5. Upright.

h.

1. A shepherd.
2. Dress.
3. Thick-headed.
4. Walking on the toes.
5. A bird.
6. To ransom.

No. XI.—Word Diamonds.

Sometimes, instead of a square, the letters are required to be arranged in the form of a diamond, say, one letter in the top line, three in the second, five in the third, three in the fourth, and one in the last line, subject to the same condition—that, horizontally or vertically, they shall read alike. The following are examples:—

a.

1. A single letter.
2. The juice of the olive.
3. Fir trees.
4. A meadow.
5. A single letter.

b.

1. A single letter.
2. A garden tool.
3. Substantives.
4. An extremity.
5. A single letter.

c.
1. A single letter.
2. The cry of a sheep.
3. A sweetmeat.
4. A girl's name.
5. A single letter.

d.
1. A vowel.
2. An animal.
3. Eve's bane.
4. A tree.
5. A vowel.

e.
1. A consonant.
2. The ocean.
3. Arab dwellings.
4. Consumed.
5. A consonant.

f.
1. A single letter.
2. Smoked pig-meat.
3. A male Christian name.
4. The title of a married lady.
5. A single letter.

g.
1. A consonant.
2. To place.
3. A fruit.
4. An adverb denoting excess.
5. A consonant.

h.
1. A consonant.
2. A feature.
3. A boundary.
4. A deep hole.
5. A consonant.

The next pair are a trifle more elaborate, the longest word having seven, instead of five, letters.

i.
1. A consonant.
2. A point.
3. The Papal crown.
4. A precious stone.
5. Haughty.
6. A conjunction.
7. A consonant.

j.
1. A consonant.
2. Phœbus.
3. Tasty.
4. Jove.
5. Saltpetre.
6. A river.
7. A consonant.

In the next pair the longest word is of *nine* letters.

k.
1. A consonant.
2. A precious stone.
3. Danger.
4. A military officer.
5. A performer of nocturnal music.
6. A marvel.
7. A long spoon.
8. Sheltered from the wind.
9. A consonant.

l.
1. A consonant.
2. Instead of.
3. Apple centres.
4. Pincers.
5. Chinaware.
6. To choose again.
7. Vacancy.
8. To occupy a seat.
9. A consonant.

No. XII.—A Cross of Diamonds.

This is an extremely ingenious puzzle. Required, to form a cross consisting of four diamonds of five words each, united in the centre by five additional letters, forming a smaller diamond, after the fashion shown in Fig. 370:—

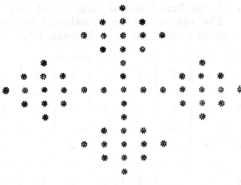

FIG. 370.

The diamond at top is to be made up as follows: 1, a single letter; 2, the queen of the fairies; 3, a title of courtesy applied to ladies; 4, wicked; 5, a single letter.

The right-hand diamond as follows: 1, a single letter; 2, past tense of a verb meaning to possess; 3, a colourless fluid; 4, the abode of a wild animal; 5, a single letter.

The left-hand diamond: 1, a single letter; 2, a fruit; 3, a flower; 4, a metal; 5, a single letter.

The bottom diamond: 1, a single letter; 2, to strike; 3, close; 4, an article; 5, a single letter.

The central diamond, read in conjunction with the bottom letter of the top diamond, the top letter of the bottom diamond, the left-hand letter of the right-hand diamond, and the right-hand letter of the left-hand diamond, will form as follows:—From centre to top, a male sheep; from centre to bottom, a small animal; from centre to right, crude; from centre to left, a quick blow; from top to centre, to deface; from bottom to centre, a resinous substance; from right to centre, open hostility; from left to centre, equal value.

Each diamond (other than that in the centre) must be perfect in itself, forming the same words both horizontally and vertically.

No. XIII.—Knight's Tour Letter Puzzles.

The principle of the "Knight's Tour" on the chessboard has been made the foundation of another and different class of puzzles. The squares of the chessboard are here occupied by letters or words (one in each square), which, if read

R	L	T	E	Y	L	R	O
Y	H	L	T	O	B	T	A
T	A	A	A		H	T	I
E	L		E	I	N	E	O
D	H	W		Y	E	S	Y
R	T	E	S	D		B	W
Y	N	E	S	N	D	A	E
H	A	A	A	W	I	D	E

A. Fig. 371.

in due sequence, according to Knight's Tour rules, form a proverb, a verse of poetry, or a well-known quotation. A (Fig. 371) is an example of this class. The letters, read aright, will be found to form a popular proverb.

B (Fig. 372), furnishes another example, and C (Fig. 373), a third.

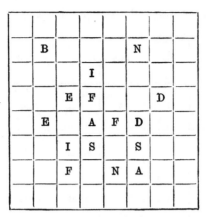

B. FIG. 372.

	B				N		
			I				
		E	F			D	
	E		A	F	D		
		I	S		S		
		F		N	A		

				E			
		E				T	
			L	H			
	E		R		S		
		E	A	S			
D		E		O		S	
			S	P		M	

C. FIG. 373.

No. XIV.—Knight's Tour Word Puzzle.

The words of the following puzzle (Fig. 374), duly read

sym-pathy	man	the	link	in	granted	body	it
is	the	the	in	be-neath	liveth	fierce	soon as
to	secret	alone	not	silver	and	fly;	in
silken,	it	given	the	soul	mind,	wishes	desire,
has	heaven	it	to	the	fan-tasy's	can	to
die;	tie	gift	not	desire	heart,	with	whose
it	God	heart	doth	hot	love's	mind	bind.
which	not	is	which	and,	dead	fire,	true

FIG. 374.

according to Knight's Tour rules, will be found to form a well-known passage from the "Lay of the Last Minstrel."

No. XV.—Hidden Proverbs.

```
R E N O W N E D T H A N W
S Y O U R C A K E A N D A
S T E T O B E F E A R H R
E A R K S S P O I L E A F
L E O O H E R S N T D V O
O T M O T L I N O H T E U
N O S C A L A G M E H I R
S N I Y G O R S O B A T S
E N G N E N O T S R N P A
I A O A M O O T S O A E W
R C D E V I L A H T D A S
O U O Y N O I L D A E C A
T C I V R E H H T A H E Z
```

The above apparent jumble contains five well-known proverbs, arranged in a systematic order. When the clue is once discovered, the proverbs can be read without difficulty.

PUZZLE : *To find it.*

No. XVI.—The Five Arab Maxims.

The subjoined table (Fig. 375), to any one who can read

never	all	forhe who	all	often	more than
tell	you may know	tells	he knows	tells	he knows
attempt	youcan do	attempts	he can do	attempts	he can do
believe	you hear	believes	he hears	believes	he hears
spend	you can afford	spends	he can afford	spends	he can afford
decide upon	you may see	decides upon	he sees	decides upon	he sees

FIG. 375.

it rightly, contains five maxims, said to be held in great esteem by the Bedouin Arabs.

KEY TO CHAPTER II.

No. I.—A Puzzling Inscription. Solution.

The letter E, which, inserted at the proper intervals, makes the inscription read as under :—

> PERSEVERE YE PERFECT MEN,
>
> EVER KEEP THESE PRECEPTS TEN.

No. II.—An Easy One.

This is a problem of the "quibble" order. The seven letters duly arranged form ONE WORD.

No. III.—Pied Proverbs. Solutions.

A. Rolling stones gather no moss.
B. Procrastination is the thief of time.
C. Time and tide wait for no man.
D. A bird in the hand is worth two in the bush.
E. All is not gold that glitters.
F. Fine words butter no parsnips.
G. Fine feathers make fine birds.
H. All's well that ends well.

No. IV.—Scattered Sentiment. Solution.

The lines should read as follows :—

> Around me shall hover,
> In sadness or glee,
> Till life's dreams be over,
> Sweet mem'ries of thee.

109

No. V.—Dropped-Letter Proverbs.

a. A stitch in time saves nine.
b. Faint heart never won fair lady.
c. Strike while the iron's hot.
d. He laughs best who laughs last.
e. Birds of a feather flock together.
f. He who goes a borrowing goes a sorrowing.
g. Children and fools speak the truth.
h. When the wine is in, the wit is out.
i. Short reckonings make long friends.
k. Honesty is the best policy.
l. A pin a day is a groat a year.
m. Take care of the pence, and the pounds will take care of themselves.

No. VI.—Dropped-Letter Nursery Rhymes.

(1) How doth the little busy bee
    Improve each shining hour;
He gathers honey all the day
    From every opening flower.

(2) Jack and Jill went up the hill
    To fetch a pail of water;
Jack fell down and broke his crown,
    And Jill came tumbling after.

(3) Hey diddle diddle, the cat and the fiddle,
    The cow jumped over the moon,
The little dog laughed to see such fine sport,
    And the dish ran away with the spoon.

No. VII.—Transformations. Solutions.

Hand; hard; lard;* lord; ford; fort; Foot.
Sin; son; won; Woe.
Hate; have; lave; Love.
Black; slack; stack; stalk;* stale; shale; whale; while; White

---

* These are examples of a necessity, which frequently arises, of inter-

Wood; wool; cool; Coal.
Blue; bile; pile; pine; Pink.
Cat; cot; cog; Dog.
More; lore; lose; loss; Less.
Rose; lose; lost; list; lilt; Lily.
Shoe; shot; soot; Boot.

No. VIII.—Beheaded Words.

1. L–arch.
2. A–loft.
3. F–lung.
4. A–bout.
5. Y–ours.
6. E–rase.
7. T–aunt.
8. T–ease.
9. E–vent.

The initials, as will be seen, give the word LAFAYETTE.

No. IX.—Anagrams.

a. Radical reform.
b. Congregationalist.
c. Presbyterian.
d. Maidenly.
e. Felicity.
f. To run at men.
g. Made moral.
h. Spare him not.
i. Golden Land.
j. Great helps.
k. Sly ware.
l. Moon-starers.
m. No more stars.

posing a move which does not directly aid the transformation, but indirectly as a link with some more desirable word.

In the first example, the word " food " might (in place of " fort") form the intermediate step between " ford " and " foot."

No. X.—Word Squares.

a. L A N E   *b.* N O N E
    A R E A   O V E R
    N E A R   N E A R
    E A R S   E R R S

c. L A M E   *d.* L O A D
    A R I D   O U S E
    M I N E   A S K S
    E D E N   D E S K

e. D O L L   *f.* R O M E
    O H I O   O P A L
    L I O N   M A U L
    L O N E   E L L A

g. W A S T E   *h.* P A S T O R
    A C T O R   A T T I R E
    S T O N E   S T U P I D
    T O N I C   T I P T O E
    E R E C T   O R I O L E
                   R E D E E M

No. XI.—Word Diamonds. Solutions.

In solving puzzles of this class, endeavour, if the indications be sufficient, to guess the centre or key word. Arrange this word in the form of a cross, thus—

$$
\begin{array}{c}
\text{P} \\
\text{I} \\
\text{P I N E S.} \\
\text{E} \\
\text{S}
\end{array}
$$

If you have guessed rightly so far, the discovery of the remaining words is a comparatively easy matter.

If the indication given as to the key word is too vague to guide you, endeavour to discover one or both of the next longest words, which will frequently give a clue to the principal word.

a.
```
      P
    O I L
  P I N E S
    L E A
      S
```

b.
```
      N
    H O E
  N O U N S
    E N D
      S
```

c.
```
      C
    B A A
  C A N D Y
    A D A
      Y
```

d.
```
      A
    A P E
  A P P L E
    E L M
      E
```

e.
```
      T
    S E A
  T E N T S
    A T E
      S
```

f.
```
      H
    H A M
  H A R R Y
    M R S
      Y
```

g.
```
      M
    S E T
  M E L O N
    T O O
      N
```

h.
```
      L
    L I P
  L I M I T
    P I T
      T
```

i.
```
        D
      T I P
    T I A R A
  D I A M O N D
    P R O U D
      A N D
        D
```

j.
```
        J
      S U N
    S A P I D
  J U P I T E R
    N I T R E
      D E E
        R
```

```
k.        S              l.              P
        G E M                          F O R
      P E R I L                      C O R E S
      G E N E R A L                F O R C E P S
    S E R E N A D E R    ·      P O R C E L A I N
      M I R A C L E              R E E L E C T
        L A D L E                  S P A C E
          L E E                      S I T
            R                          N
```

No. XII.—A Cross of Diamonds. Solution.

```
                    M
                  M A B
                M A D A M
                  B A D
          T       M       W
        N U T      A     H A D
      T U L I P A R A W A T E R
        T I N      A     D E N
          P        T       R
                  H I T
                T I G H T
                  T H E
                    T
```

No. XIII.—Knight's Tour Letter Puzzles.
Solution.

A. Fig. 376 indicates the order in which the letters are to be taken, when they will be found to read as follows :—

"Early to bed and early to rise
Is the way to be healthy, and wealthy, and wise."

3	40	19	36	5	50	21	34
18	37	4	51	20	35	6	49
41	2	39	54		52	33	22
38	17		1	58	55	48	7
13	42	57		53	60	23	32
16	27	14	59	56		8	47
43	12	29	26	45	10	31	24
28	15	44	11	30	25	46	9

FIG. 376.

In B the order of the letters is as shown in Fig. 377, the hidden proverb being, "Safe bind, safe find."

	5				7		
			6				
		4	13			8	
	12		10	3	16		
		14	1		9		
		11		15	2		

FIG. 377.

In C the order is as shown in Fig. 378, and the proverb, "More haste, less speed."

				9			
		4				8	
			10	5			
	17		3		7		
		11	6	13			
18		16		2		14	
			12	15		1	

Fig. 378.

No. XIV.—The Knight's Tour Word Puzzle.
Solution.

43	10	41	46	29	24	59	26
40	47	44	61	12	27	30	23
9	42	11	28	45	60	25	58
48	39	8	13	62	57	22	31
7	14	35	52	3	18	63	56
38	49	4	17	34	53	32	21
15	6	51	36	19	2	55	64
50	37	16	5	54	33	20	1

FIG. 379.

The key to this puzzle will be found in Fig. 379. Read according to the order here indicated, it will be found that the words make the following stanza:—

" True love's the gift which God has given
    To man alone beneath the heaven:
        It is not fantasy's hot fire,
            Whose wishes, soon as granted, fly;
        It liveth not in fierce desire,
            With dead desire it doth not die:
    It is the secret sympathy,
    The silver link, the silken tie,
    Which heart to heart, and mind to mind,
    In body and in soul can bind."
                    Lay of the Last Minstrel. Canto V.

The construction of other problems on the same model will be found very interesting. Should the passage used be less than the full number of sixty-four words, a word may here and there be cut in two, so as to occupy two squares, or the superfluous squares may be left unoccupied. If the quotation be too long, two words may be made to occupy a single square, like "soon as" in the example given.

No. XV.—Hidden Proverbs. Solution.

The five proverbs are as follows :—
   A rolling stone gathers no moss.
   Too many cooks spoil the broth.
   A live dog is more to be feared than a dead lion.
   You cannot eat your cake and have it.
   Peace hath her victories, no less renowned than war.

To read them, first find the central letter, which is A. This begins the first proverb. Immediately below this will be found R, to the left of this O, and above the O two L's. To the right of the last L are the letters I N. The G, completing the word "rolling," comes next below the N, and below this, S, the initial of the next word, "stone." From the S, moving to the left, we have the remaining letters, T O N E, and so we read on, following the course of the sun, round each square of letters in succession.

For greater clearness we exhibit separately the central square and a few letters of the next square, showing the commencement of the process.

```
    L  I  N
    L  A  G
    O  R  S
 E  N  O  T
```

No. XVI.—The Five Arab Maxims. Solution.

The key to this puzzle consists in reading first the words in the first and second lines alternately. Then those in the first and third alternately. Then in the first and fourth, the first and fifth, and first and sixth in succession. The maxims will then be found to run as follows :—

"Never tell all you know ; for he who tells all he knows, often tells more than he knows."

"Never attempt all you can do; for he who attempts all he can do often attempts more than he can do."

"Never believe all you hear, for he who believes," etc., etc.

And so on, the words in the first line being common to each maxim.

CHAPTER III.

PUZZLES of this class are frequently propounded in more or less fanciful forms,—*e.g.*, a gardener is required to plant trees, or an officer to place his men, in such manner as to answer the conditions of the problem. From considerations of space, we have thought it best to leave such fanciful elaborations for the most part to the imagination of the reader. Should he prefer to put the question in such a shape, he will have little difficulty in inventing an appropriate legend.

No. I.

Required, to arrange eleven counters in such manner that they shall form twelve rows, with three counters in each row.

No. II.

Required, to arrange nine counters in such manner that they shall form ten rows, with three counters in each row.

No. III.

Required, to arrange twenty-seven counters in such manner as to form nine rows, with six counters in each row.

No. IV.

Required, to arrange ten counters in such manner that they shall form five rows, with four counters in each row.

No. V.

Required, to arrange twelve counters in such manner that they shall make six rows of four counters each.

No. VI.

Required, to arrange nineteen counters in such manner that they shall form nine rows of five counters each.

No. VII.

Required, to arrange sixteen counters so as to form ten rows, with four counters in each row.

No. VIII.

Required, to arrange twelve counters in such manner that they shall count four in a straight line in seven different directions.

No. IX.

Required, to arrange nine white and nine red counters in such manner that there shall be ten rows, of three counters each, *white*, and eight rows of three each *red*.

No. X.

Given, a square, divided into nine smaller squares. Required, to arrange counters in the eight outer squares in such manner that there shall always be nine on each side of the square, though the total be repeatedly varied, being 24, 20, 28, 32, and 36 in succession.

This is a very ancient problem. It is usually propounded after the fashion following : A blind abbot was at the head

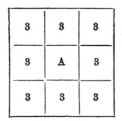

FIG. 380.

of a monastery of twenty-four monks, who were domiciled three in a cell in eight cells, occupying the four sides of a square, while the abbot himself occupied a cell in the centre. To assure himself that all were duly housed for the night, he was in the habit of visiting the cells at frequent intervals, and counting the occupants, reckoning that if he found nine monks in each row of three cells (see Fig. 380), the tale was complete.

But the brethren succeeded in eluding his vigilance. First

four of them absented themselves (reducing the number to twenty), but still the abbot counted and found nine in a row. Then these four returned, bringing four friends with them, thus making twenty-eight persons, and yet the normal nine in a row was not increased. Presently four more outsiders came in, making thirty-two. The result was the same. Again, four more visitors arrived, making a total of thirty-six, but the abbot, going his rounds, found nine persons in each row as before.

How was this managed?

No. XI.

Required, so to place ten counters that they shall count four in a row in eight different directions.

No. XII.

Required, so to place thirteen counters that they shall count five in a straight line in twelve different directions.

No. XIII.

This is a puzzle of a different character.

Given, an eight-pointed star, as shown in Fig. 381, and seven counters. You are required to place the counters on

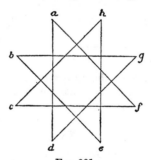

Fig. 381.

seven of the points of the star, in so doing strictly following the rule following—viz., Each counter is to be drawn from a vacant point along the corresponding line to another vacant point, and there left. You then start from another vacant point, and proceed in like manner till the seven points are covered.

No. XIV.—The "Okto" Puzzle.

The puzzle brought out under this name is a variation on the foregoing. Each point of the star terminates in a small circle, on which is printed the name of a given colour—black, yellow, carmine, and so on. The counters, eight in number, are of corresponding colours. The aspirant is required to cover seven of the circles, according to the rule laid down for the last puzzle, each with the counter of its proper colour.

No. XV.

Given, the figure described in Fig. 382.

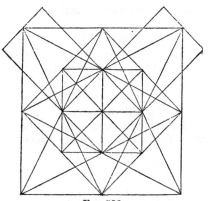

Fɪɢ. 382.

Required, to place at the intersections of its various lines twenty-one counters, in such manner as to form thirty rows of three counters each, each group of three being united by one of the lines.

No. XVI.

This is sometimes known as the "crowning" puzzle. The reader will remember that at the game of draughts a man reaching the opposite side of the board becomes a king, and is "crowned" by having a second man placed on the top of it. In the case of the puzzle we are about to describe ten counters, or men, are placed in a row, and the player is required to "crown" five of them after the following fashion. He is to take up one counter, pass it to right or left *over two others*, and crown the one next in order, proceeding in like manner till the whole are crowned.

A king, it should be stated, is still regarded as being *two* counters.

No. XVII.—The " Right and Left " Puzzle.

This is a very excellent puzzle, and has the special recommendation of being very little known. Rule on cardboard a rectangular figure consisting of seven equal spaces, each one inch square (see Fig. 383). In the three spaces to the left place three red, and in the three spaces to the right three white counters, the space in the middle being left unoccupied.

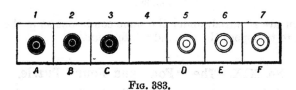

Fig. 383.

The puzzle is to transpose the red and white counters, so that the three white shall be in the left hand, and the three red in the right hand spaces. This is to be done in accordance with the following conditions, viz. :—

1. Each counter can only be moved one space at a time.

2. If a counter is divided from a vacant space by a single counter only, it may pass over it into such vacant space.

3. Counters may only be moved in a *forward* direction—*i.e.*, red to the right, and white to the left. A move once made cannot be retracted.

No. XVIII.

This is a further development of the same problem. Rule a sheet of paper into squares so that each horizontal row shall contain seven, and each vertical row five, and upon them place red and white counters (17 of each colour), as shown in the diagram* (Fig. 384), the central space (No. 18) being left vacant.

---

* If preferred, one corner of a draught- or gobang-board may be used, in place of the ruled paper.

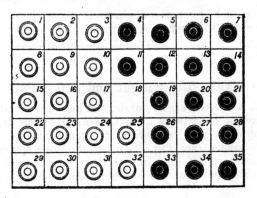

FIG. 384.

You are required, under the same conditions as in the last case, to transpose the red and white counters. ·

No. XIX.—The "Four and Four" Puzzle.

This is in general idea very similar to the two puzzles last described, but it is wholly different in working.

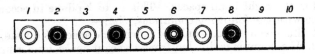

FIG. 385.

Rule on cardboard a rectangular figure, divided into ten squares, as Fig. 385, and in the first eight spaces, beginning from the left hand, dispose eight counters, red and black alternately.

The puzzle is, moving them *two at a time*, to get the four

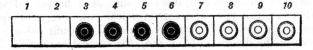

FIG. 386.

red and the four black counters grouped each colour together without any interval, and this must be done *in four mores only.* At the close of the operation the eight counters should be as shown in Fig. 386.

They are then to be worked back again, after the same fashion, to their original positions.

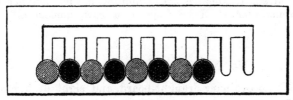

FIG. 387.

This puzzle is sometimes arranged in the form of a slip of wood, seven inches by two, with its central portion cut out with a fret-saw, as shown in Fig. 387. The counters are here replaced by little blocks of wood, each in the shape of a collar-stud. They may be shifted backwards and forwards from gap to gap with great ease, but cannot be detached from the board, and are therefore always available for use.

No. XX.—The "Five and Five" Puzzle.

This is the same as that last described, save that *ten* counters, five of each colour, are used, and that the desired transposition is to be effected in *five* moves.

No. XXI.—The "Six and Six" Puzzle.

This is again the same problem, but with *twelve* counters, six of each colour, the transposition to be effected in *six* moves.

No. XXII.—The Thirty-six Puzzle.

Thirty-six counters are arranged in the form of a square, six rows of six each.

Required, to remove six counters in such manner that the remaining counters shall still have an even number in each row, horizontal and vertical.

No. XXIII.—The "Five to Four" Puzzle.

Twenty-five counters are arranged in the form of a square, five rows of five each.

Required, to remove five counters in such manner that the remainder shall be four in a row, horizontally and vertically.

No. XXIV.—No Two in a Row.

With an ordinary draught-board, and eight draughtsmen or counters.

Required, so to dispose the eight men upon various squares of the board that no two shall be in the same line, either vertically, horizontally, or diagonally.

No. XXV.—The "Simple" Puzzle.

A further and very interesting development of the last-mentioned "poser" has been brought out, under the name

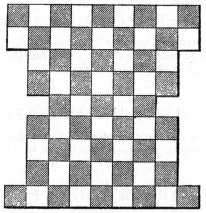

Fig. 388.

of the "Simple" Puzzle, by Messrs. Feltham. Simple as it may be, in a sense, we have known much keen thought expended upon it before the coveted solution was obtained.

A special board of 67 squares is used, arranged as shown in Fig. 388, and the problem is to place *nine* counters upon it, in accordance with the conditions of the last puzzle.

N.B.—It should be stated that the indentations on either side of the board do not affect the conditions. Thus, two counters placed respectively in the left hand top and bottom corner squares would be regarded as being in the same line, notwithstanding that there is a break of continuity between them.

No. XXVI.—The " English Sixteen " Puzzle.

A clever puzzle, under the above title, is issued by Messrs. Heywood, of Manchester. In the result to be attained it is almost identical with No. XVIII. (p. 269), but the conditions are in this case somewhat different, and the puzzle considerably more difficult.

A board, as illustrated in Fig. 389, is used, with eight

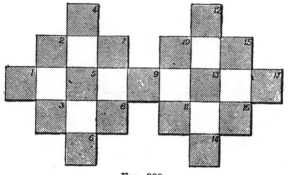

FIG. 389.

white and eight red counters. These are arranged on the *black* squares, the red to the right, the white to the left, the central square, No. 9 in the figure, being left vacant. The problem, as in the puzzle above-mentioned, is to transpose the red and white counters, the men to be moved according to " draughts " rules—*i.e.*, forward only; the whites towards the spaces occupied by the reds, and the reds towards the spaces occupied by the whites. The men move only on the black squares, and therefore diagonally. A white man can pass over a black man, or a black man over a white man, provided that the space next beyond is vacant.

No. XXVII.—The Twenty Counters.

Required, (a) so to arrange twenty counters as to form therewith thirteen different squares.

(b) To remove six counters only from the figure formed as above, so that no single square shall remain.

KEY TO CHAPTER III.

N.B.—It must not be taken for granted, in the case of puzzles which demand a particular arrangement of counters, that the solution given is the only one possible, as there may frequently be two or more modes of arrangement which will equally answer the conditions of the problem.

No. I.—Solution.

The eleven counters are arranged as shown in Fig. 390.

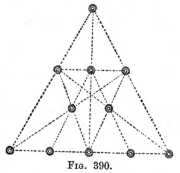

FIG. 390.

The five at bottom count as two rows of three, the counter in the middle being common to both.

No. II.—Solution.

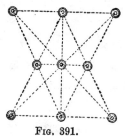

FIG. 391.

Arrange the nine counters as shown in Fig. 391.

131

No. III.—Solution.

There are several different arrangements which will

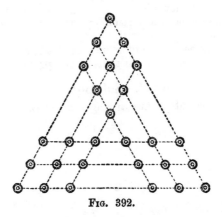

Fig. 392.

answer the conditions of this problem. Figs. 392 and 393 represent two of such arrangements.

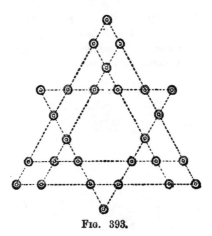

Fig. 393.

No. IV.—Solution.

This again may be solved in various ways.   Either of

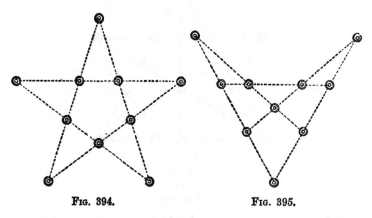

FIG. 394.   FIG. 395.

the subjoined arrangements (Figs. 394 and 395) will answer
the required conditions.

No. V.— Solution.

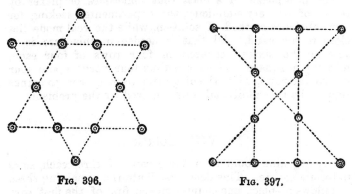

FIG. 396.   FIG. 397.

The counters may be arranged as shown in Fig. 396 or
Fig. 397.

No. VI.—Solution.

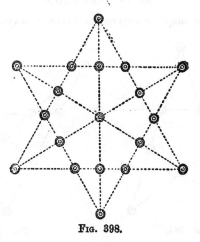

FIG. 398.

The nineteen counters should be arranged as shown in Fig. 398.

No. VII.—Solution.

This is a puzzle of a class that sometimes perplexes by reason of its very simplicity, the experimenter seeking for some abstruse method of solution, while the real mode lies close to his hand. All that is needed in this case is to arrange the sixteen counters in four rows of four each, forming a square. There are thus four vertical and four horizontal rows, while the diagonals from corner to corner supply the two additional rows required by the problem.

No. VIII.—Solution.

Lay out nine counters in three rows of three each, so as to form a square. This done, distribute the remaining three as follows :—place one counter on the first of the first row, another on the second of the second row, and the third on the last of the third row.

No. IX.—**Solution.**

The counters must be arranged as in the subjoined dia-

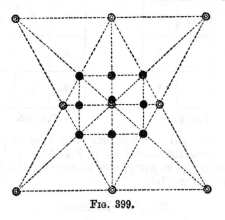

Fig. 399.

gram (Fig. 399). Note that the centre counter is duplica-
ted, a red counter lying half over a white counter, or *vice
versâ*, so as to do double duty.

No. X.—**Solution.**

The secret lies in increasing or diminishing, as the case
may require, the number of persons in the corner cells,

4	1	4
1		1
4	1	4

Fig. 400.

2	5	2
5		5
2	5	2

Fig. 401.

each of which counts twice over, and so, to a person as
doddering as the abbot must be assumed to have been,
seems at first sight to increase the general total. Thus

when the four monks absented themselves, the remaining
twenty were re-arranged as in Fig. 400; and when they
returned with four other persons, the twenty-eight were dis-

1	7	1
7		7
1	7	1

0	9	0
9		9
0	9	0

Fig. 402.   Fig. 403.

posed as in Fig. 401. When four more visitors arrived, the
thirty-two were distributed as in Fig. 402; and when the
final four arrived, the party, now numbering thirty-six, were
arranged as in Fig. 403.

No. XI.—Solution.

This is a quibble dependent on the special wording of the
problem. You begin by distributing the counters in three
rows of three each, forming a square, and then place the
remaining counter on the centre one. You have now four
rows of four each; but as each row can be counted in two
different directions—*i.e.*, from right to left or left to right,
and vertical rows upwards or downwards—you are enabled
to count four in eight different directions, as required by the
problem.

No. XII.—Solution.

This is effected on a similar principle. You arrange nine of
the counters in three rows of three each, forming a square
as above described, and place the remaining four one on
each of the four " corner " counters. This gives you six
rows of five each, enabling you to count five in twelve
different directions.

No. XIII.—Solution.

The secret lies in working backwards throughout, each
time covering the point from which you last started. Thus,
placing a counter on *a*, draw it along the line *a d*, and leave

it on *d*. *a* is now the next point to be covered, and there is only one vacant line, *f a*, which leads to it. Place, therefore, your second counter on *f*, draw it along *f a*, and leave it on *a*. The third counter must be placed on *c*, drawn along *c f*, and left on *f*. The next placed on *h*, and left on *c*. The fifth is placed on *e*, and left on *h*. The sixth is placed on *b*, and left on *e*; and the seventh placed on *g*, and left on *b*.

You now have the whole seven counters duly placed, and only one point, *g*, left uncovered.

No. XIV.—The "Okto" Puzzle. Solution.

The requirement in this case that each circle shall be covered with a counter of a given colour does not in reality add anything to the difficulty of the puzzle, though it appears to do so to any one attempting it for the first time. The experimenter has only to proceed as indicated in the last solution, taking care in each case to use the counter corresponding in colour with the circle on which he proposes to leave it.

No. XV.—Solution.

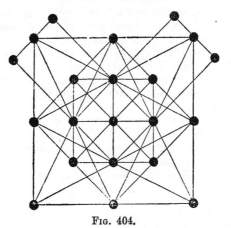

Fig. 404.

The counters must be placed as shown in Fig. 404.

No. XVI.—**Solution.**

Supposing the row of counters to be indicated from left to right by numbers as under—

1, 2, 3, 4, 5, 6, 7, 8, 9, 10.

Proceed as follows :—

Place 4 on 1, 6 on 9, 8 on 3, 2 on 5, and 10 on 7.

or

Place 4 on 1, 7 on 3, 5 on 9, 2 on 6, and 10 on 8.

There are several formulas which will answer the problem, but a person trying the puzzle for the first time will find some difficulty in hitting upon one of them.

No. XVII.—**The " Right and Left" Puzzle. Solution.**

The key to this puzzle lies in the observance of the following rules :—

1. After having moved a counter, one *of the opposite colour* must invariably be passed over it.

2. After having passed one counter over another, the next advance will be *with the same colour* as such first-mentioned counter. The position will guide you whether to move or to pass over, only one of such alternatives being usually open to you.

The above rules, however, only apply up to a certain point. After the ninth move you will find that the next should be with a counter of the same colour; but none such is available. By this time, however, the puzzle is practically solved. The counters are white and red alternately, with the space to the extreme left vacant, and two or three obvious moves place the counters so as to answer the conditions of the problem.

Thus, if we begin with the white counters, the moves will be as under (see Fig. 383), the spaces being designated by the numbers, and the counters by the letters :—

1. *D* moves into space 4.
2. *C* passes over *D* into space 5.
3. *B* moves into space 3.
4. *D* passes over *B* into space 2.
5. *E* passes over *C* into space 4.
6. *F* moves into space 6.
7. *C* passes over *F* into space 7.

8. *B* passes over *E* into space 5.

9. *A* passes over *D* into space 3.

Here occurs the state of things to which we have referred the position being as in Fig. 405.

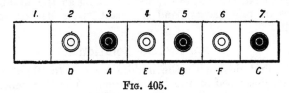

Fig. 405.

The next move should, according to the rule, be with a red counter; but there is only one counter, and that a white one, *D*, which is capable of being moved in a forward direction, and that *only* into 1. This move is made accordingly, and the solution proceeds as follows, the remaining moves being almost a matter of course:—

10. *D* moves into space 1.

11. *E* passes over *A* into space 2.

12. *F* passes over *B* into space 4.

13. *B* moves into space 6.

14. *A* passes over *F* into space 5.

15. *F* moves into space 3, and the trick is done.

If the operator prefers to begin with the *red* counters, the moves will be as follows :—

1. *C* moves into 4.

2. *D* passes over into 3.

3. *E* moves into 5.

4. *C* passes over into 6.

5. *B* passes over into 4.

6. *A* moves into 2.

7. *D* passes over into 1.

8. *E* passes over into 3.

9. *F* passes over into 5.

(From this point, as before, the rule ceases to apply.)

10. *C* moves into 7.

11. *B* passes over into 6.

12. *A* passes over into 4.

13. *E* moves into 2.

14. *F* passes over into 3.

15. *A* moves into 5.

When the principle is once fairly mastered, the movements can be executed with great rapidity, and with little fear of any onlooker being able to repeat them from recollection.

The solution we have given is equally applicable to any larger (even) number of counters, so long as the number of spaces be one greater, and a vacant space be left in the middle.

No. XVIII.—Solution.

You first deal with the middle row (15 to 21) after the manner described in the last solution. You then move the white counter now occupying space 25 into the central space (18), and deal in like manner with the fourth row (22 to 28), leaving space 25 vacant. Pass the counter occupying 11 into this space, and you are then in a position to deal with the second row (8 to 14). When space 11 is again vacant, move the counter occupying space 4 into it, and you are then enabled to deal with the uppermost line (1 to 7).

Pass the counter occupying space 18 into space 4, and that occupying space 32 into space 18. You are now in a position to rearrange the last row (29 to 35). You have then a vacant space (32) in the centre of the bottom row. Move the counter occupying space 25 into this space, then pass that occupying 11 into 25, and finally move the counter now in 18 into 11.

No. XIX.—The "Four and Four" Puzzle. Solution.

The necessary transpositions are as follows :—

Shift the counters occupying spaces 2 and 3 to 9 and 10 ;

”	”	”	”	5 and 6 „ 2 and 3 ;
”	”	”	”	8 and 9 „ 5 and 6 ;
”	”	”	”	1 and 2 „ 8 and 9.

To work the counters back again, you have merely to reverse the process, but to do this from memory is rather more difficult than the original puzzle, and some amount of practice is necessary before it can be done with facility.

No. XX.—The "Five and Five" Puzzle. Solution.

For the sake of brevity, we will distinguish the red and black counters by the letters *r* and *b* respectively. They will then stand at the outset as under :—

                                b r b r b r b r b r . .
Position after 1st move : *b* . . *r b r b r b r r b*
   „   „ 2nd „ *b b r r b r* . . *b r r b*
   „   „ 3rd „ *b b r* . . *r r b b r r b*
   „   „ 4th „ *b b r r r r r b b* . . *b*
   „   „ 5th „ . . *r r r r r b b b b b*

N.B.—Where the number of pairs is *odd*, the second move should be with the pair next following that in the centre.

No. XXI.—The " Six and Six " Puzzle. Solution.

Distinguishing the counters as before, we have at the outset :—

                                b r b r b r b r b r b r . .
Position after 1st move : *b* . . *r b r b r b r b r r b*
   „   „ 2nd „ *b b r r* . . *b r b r b r r b*
   „   „ 3rd „ *b b r r r b b r b* . . *r r b*
   „   „ 4th „ *b b r r* . . *r b b b r r b*
   „   „ 5th „ *b b r r r r r r b b b* . . *b*
   „   „ 6th „ . . *r r r r r r b b b b b b*

No. XXII.—The Thirty-Six Puzzle. Solution.

Fig. 406.

The six counters are so removed as to leave the remainder as under (Fig. 406).

No. XXIII.—The " Five to Four " Puzzle. Solution.

Remove the five counters of either diagonal, when those remaining will be found to answer the conditions of the problem.

No. XXIV.—No Two in a Row. Solution.

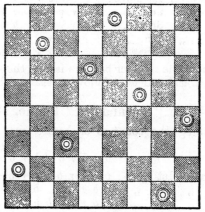

Fig. 407.

Arrange the eight draughtsmen, or counters, as shown in Fig. 407.

No. XXV.—The "Simple" Puzzle. Solution.

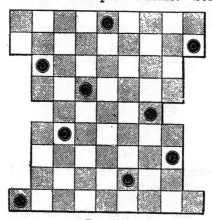

Fig. 408.

The arrangement of the nine counters is as shown in Fig. 408.

No. XXVI.—The "English Sixteen" Puzzle. Solution.

We know of no rule for working this puzzle. There are several possible solutions. Among others, moving the men in the following order will be found to answer the conditions of the problem. The man to be moved is in each case indicated by the number of the square (see Fig. 389). It is not necessary to specify the square to which it is to be moved. As there is never more than one square vacant, the experimenter cannot well go wrong in this particular.

It will be observed that the number of moves is 52, which we believe to be the smallest which will suffice to transfer the whole of the men.

11,   7,   9,   8,   10, 13, 11, 14, 9,   6,   8,   5,   7,

11,   9,   10, 8,   2,   1,   6,   3,   5,   7,   4,   9,   12,

15, 17, 14, 16, 13, 15, 11,   7, 9, 14, 11, 13, 10,

8,   9,   6,   8,   2,   5,   7,   11, 9, 12, 10, 8,   9.

No. XXVII.—"The Twenty Counters." Solution.

(*a*) If the counters be arranged as shown in Fig. 409, it will be found that they form seventeen perfect squares.

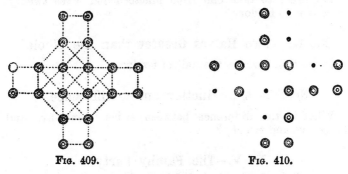

FIG. 409.   FIG. 410.

(*b*) Fig. 410 shows the same arrangement of counters, less six removed. Not a single square now remains.

CHAPTER IV.

"QUIBBLE" OR "CATCH" PUZZLES.

THE present Chapter will be devoted to puzzles which depend upon some double meaning or non-natural interpretation of the question, whereby it assumes a second and less obvious signification.

No. I.—A Remarkable Division.

A gentleman divided seven and sixpence between two fathers and two sons, each father and each son receiving half a crown. How did he manage it?

No. II.—Subtraction Extraordinary.

Required, to take one from nineteen and leave twenty. How is it to be done?

No. III.—Two Halves Greater than the Whole.

Prove that seven is the half of twelve.

No. IV.—A Distinction and a Difference.

What is the difference between twice twenty-five and twice five and twenty?

No. V.—The Family Party.

A family gathering included 1 grandfather, 1 grandmother, 2 fathers, 2 mothers, 4 children, 3 grandchildren, 1 brother, 2 sisters, 2 sons, 2 daughters, 1 father-in-law, 1 mother-in-law, and 1 daughter-in-law, and yet there were only seven persons present.

How can the two statements be reconciled?

144

No. VI.—A Sum in Subtraction.

What is the difference between six dozen dozen and half a dozen dozen ?

No. VII.—Another Sum in Subtraction.

What is the difference in capacity between twenty four quart bottles and four-and-twenty quart bottles ?

No. VIII.—Three Times Six.

Place three sixes together so as to make seven.

No. IX.—A New Way of Writing 100.

Required, to express 100 by repetition of the same figure six times over.

No. X.—A Seeming Impossibility.

Required, to find six times thirteen in twelve.

No. XI.—Multiplication Extraordinary.

What three figures, multiplied by five, will make six ?

No. XII.—A Question in Notation.

How would you write in figures twelve thousand twelve hundred and twelve ?

No. XIII.—The Miraculous Herrings.

Five herrings were divided among five persons. Each had a herring, and yet one remained in the dish.
How was this managed ?

No. XIV.—Two Evens make an Odd.

Prove that two sixes make eleven.

No. XV.—Six made Three.

Out of six chalk or pencil strokes—thus, | | | | | |
to make three, without striking out or rubbing out any.

No. XVI.—A Singular Subtraction.

Required, to take ten from ten so that ten shall remain.

No. XVII.—A Sum in Addition.

Required, to add 2 to 191 and make the total less than 20.

No. XVIII.—The Flying Sixpence.

A sixpence being placed in each hand, and the arms extended shoulder high, required, to bring both coins into one hand without allowing the arms to approach each other.

No. XIX.—The Last Thing Out.

You undertake to show another person something which you never saw before, which he never saw before, and which, after you both have seen it, no one else will ever see again.

How is it to be done?

No. XX.—The Three Gingerbread Nuts.

This is propounded in the shape of a conjuring-trick, usually after two or three *bonâ-fide* tricks have been performed. You place three gingerbread nuts* on the table, and cover each with a borrowed hat. You make a great point of having nothing concealed in your hands, and profess your willingness to allow the audience, if they please, to mark the three articles, so that there can be no question of substitution.

You then take up each hat in succession, pick up the nut beneath it, and gravely eat it, replacing the hat mouth downward on the table. Any one is at liberty to see that there is nothing left under either hat. You then undertake to

---

* In default of gingerbread nuts, three almonds, raisins, or any other small eatable articles may be substituted.

bring the three nuts under whichever of the three hats the company may select; and the choice being made, you at once do so.

How is it to be done?

No. XXI.—The Mysterious Obstacle.

You undertake to clasp a person's hands in such manner that he cannot leave the room without unclasping them.

How is it to be done?

No. XXII.—The Bewitched Right Hand.

You undertake to put something into a person's left hand which he cannot possibly take in his right.

How is it to be done?

No. XXIII.—The Invisible Candle.

You undertake to place a lighted candle in such a position that it shall be visible to every person save one; such person not to be blindfolded, or prevented from turning about in any manner he pleases.

How is it to be done?

No. XXIV.—The Draper's Puzzle.

A draper, dividing a piece of cloth into yard lengths, found that he cut off one yard per second. The piece of cloth was 60 yards in length.

How long did it take him to cut up the whole?

No. XXV.—The Portrait.

A portrait hung in a gentleman's library. He was asked whom it represented. He replied,—

"Uncles and brothers have I none,
But that man's father is my father's son."

What relation was the subject of the portrait to the speaker?

No. XXVI.—The Charmed Circle.

You invite a gentleman to stand in the middle of the room. Taking a piece of chalk, you undertake to draw round him a circle which he cannot jump out of.

How is it to be done?

No. XXVII.—The Egg and the Cannon-ball.

Exhibiting an egg and a cannon-ball, you hold forth learnedly on the extraordinary strength of a perfect arch, and, still more, of a perfect dome, remarking that few people know how strong even the shell of an egg is, if it is placed in a proper position. In proof of your assertion, you undertake to place the egg, without covering it in any way, in such a position that no one present can break it with the cannon-ball.

How is it to be done?

No. XXVIII.—A Curious Window.

A window in a certain house has recently been made twice its original size, but without increasing either its height or width.

How can that be?

No. XXIX.—A Queer Calculation.

A hundred and one by fifty divide,
And next let a cipher be duly applied;
Then, if the result you should rightly divine,
You'll find that the whole makes but one out of nine.

No. XXX.—Arithmetical Enigma.

Write down a cipher, prefix fifty, to the right place five, and to the whole add one-fifth of eight. The result will give you the most important factor in human happiness.

No. XXXI.—A Short Year.

The year 1892 was one of the shortest on record.
How do you prove it?

No. XXXII.—The Mysterious Addition.

1. I add one to five, and make it four.
How can that be ?
2. What must I add to nine to make it six ?

No. XXXIII.—Arithmetical Enigma.

From a number that's odd cut off its head,
    It then will *even* be ;
Its tail, I pray, next take away,
    Your mother then you'll see.

No. XXXIV.—A New Valuation.

If five times four are thirty-three,
What will the fourth of twenty be ?

No. XXXV.—Easy, when You Know It.

What two numbers multiplied together will produce
seven ?

No. XXXVI.—Necessity the Mother of Invention.

I have a bottle of wine, corked in the ordinary way.
Unfortunately, I have no corkscrew.
How can I get the wine out, without breaking the glass, or
making a hole in the cork ?

No. XXXVII.—A Singular Subtraction.

From six take nine, from nine take ten, from forty take
fifty, and yet have six left.
How is it to be done ?

No. XXXVIII.—A Vanishing Number.

There is a number of three figures, in value not very far
short of a thousand, but when halved its value is nothing.
What is it ?

No. XXXIX.—A Queer Query.

Twice ten are six of us,
Six are but three of us,
Nine are but four of us ;
    What can we possibly be?
Would you know more of us,
Twelve are but six of us,
    Five are but four, do you see ?

No. XL.—The Mouse.

A mouse found in a box a number of ears of corn, and set to work to carry them off to his hole. He brought out with him three ears at each journey, and it took him nine journeys to remove the whole.

How many ears of corn were there in the box ?

No. XLI.—The Fasting Man.

How many hard-boiled eggs can a hungry man eat on an empty stomach ?

No. XLII.—The Family Party.

An old gentleman was asked who dined with him on Christmas Day. "Well, we were quite a family party," he replied ; "there was my father's brother-in-law, my brother's father-in-law, my father-in-law's brother-in-law, and my brother-in-law's father-in-law."

It afterwards transpired that he had dined alone, and yet his statement was correct.

How could that be ?

No. XLIII.—A Reversible Fraction.

Required, to find a fraction whose numerator is less than its denominator, but which, reversed, shall remain of the same value.

No. XLIV.—The Three Counters.

Three counters are laid in a row on the table.
Required, to take the middle one away from the middle without touching it.

No. XLV.—Magic Made Easy.

Borrow a half-crown and a penny, and hold them one in each hand, with the hands open, in front of you, the hands being about two feet apart. Now close the hands, and announce that you will make the coins change places without again opening your hands, which you proceed to do accordingly.
How is it done ?

KEY TO CHAPTER IV.

No. I.—A Remarkable Division. Solution.

There were only three persons who shared in the gift, related to each other as son, father, and grandfather. Each is necessarily a son (of somebody), while the two elder are fathers also.

No. II.—Subtraction Extraordinary. Solution.

Write nineteen in Roman numerals—XIX. Remove the I., and you have XX.

No. III.—Two Halves Greater than the Whole. Solution.

Write twelve in Roman numerals—XII. Halve the number by drawing a line horizontally across its centre, and the upper half is VII.

No. IV.—A Distinction and a Difference. Solution.

There is a difference of twenty; twice twenty-five being fifty, while twice five, and twenty, make thirty only.

No. V.—The Family Party. Solution.

The party consisted of three children (two girls and a boy), their father and mother, and their father's father and mother. It will be found that these, in their various relations to each other, fill all the characters named. Thus the father, in relation to his own father, is also a son, and so on.

No. VI.—A Sum in Subtraction. Solution.

The former are six gross, the latter six dozen only. The difference is therefore $864 - 72 = 792$.

No. VII.—Another Sum in Subtraction. Solution.

56 quarts : twenty four-quart bottles holding 80 quarts, while four-and-twenty quart bottles hold 24 quarts only.

No. VIII.—Three times Six. Solution.

$6\frac{6}{6}$.

No. IX.—A New Way of Writing 100. Solution.

$99\frac{99}{99}$ $(=100)$.

No. X.—A Seeming Impossibility. Solution.

If you write down the numbers 1 to 12 inclusive, taking in pairs the first and last, the second and last but one, and so on, you have—

1 and 12 make 13
2 and 11 „   13
3 and 10 „   13
4 and 9   „   13
5 and 8   „   13
6 and 7   „   13

Your six thirteens are thus accounted for.

No. XI.—Multiplication Extraordinary. Solution.

Answer, $1\frac{1}{5}$. $1\frac{1}{5} \times 5 = 6$.

No. XII.—A Question in Notation. Solution.

Answer, 13212.

No. XIII.—The Miraculous Herrings. Solution.

The last of the five received his herring in the dish.

No. XIV.—Two Evens make an Odd.   Solution.

This is another of the "catches" dependent upon the use of Roman numerals.   One six (VI.) is placed above another six, but the latter in an inverted position (ΛI), the combination making XI.

No. XV.—Six made Three.   Solution.

Add the necessary lines to complete the word "three," thus
T H R E E.

No. XVI.—A Sum in Subtraction.   Solution.

The propounder of this puzzle should be wearing gloves, and the problem is solved by taking them off.   The ten fingers of the gloves are taken from the ten fingers of the hand, and the latter still remain.

No. XVII.—A Sum in Addition.   Solution.

Draw a line under the final 1, and place the 2 under it, when the result will be $19\frac{1}{2}$.

No. XVIII.—The Flying Sixpence.   Solution.

Place yourself so as to bring one hand just over the mantelpiece, and drop the coin contained in such hand upon the latter.   Then, keeping the arms still extended, turn the body round till the other hand comes over the coin.   Pick it up, and you have solved the puzzle, both coins being now in one hand.

No. XIX.—The Last Thing Out.   Solution.

The puzzle is solved by cracking a nut, showing your interlocutor the kernel, and then eating it.

No. XX.—The Three Gingerbread Nuts.   Solution.

This is a very ancient "sell," but it still finds victims. The performer's undertaking is performed by simply putting on the hat selected.   No one can deny that the three nuts are thereby brought under the hat.

No. XXI.—The Mysterious Obstacle. Solution.

You perform your undertaking by clasping the person's hands round the leg of a loo table, a piano, or other object too bulky to be dragged through the doorway.

No. XXII.—The Bewitched Right Hand. Solution.

You place in the person's left hand *his own right elbow*, which, obviously, he cannot take in his right hand.

No. XXIII.—The Invisible Candle. Solution.

You place the candlestick *upon the head* of the person who is not to see it.

No. XXIV.—The Draper's Puzzle. Solution.

It took him 59 seconds. Most people are apt to say 60, forgetting that the 59th cut separates the last two lengths, and that, therefore, a 60th is unnecessary.

No. XXV.—The Portrait. Solution.

The portrait represented the speaker's son, as will be seen after a moment's consideration. The speaker says in effect, "The father of that man is my father's son"; in which case the father of the subject must be either a brother of the speaker, or himself. He has already told us that he has no brother. He himself must therefore be the father, and the portrait represents his son.[*]

No. XXVI.—The Charmed Circle. Solution.

The circle is drawn on the clothes of the victim, round the waist.

---

[*] This venerable puzzle forms the subject of a humorous article, entitled " Prove It," in a recent number of the *Idler*. Its most amusing feature is that the writer has himself gone astray, the story proceeding on the assumption that *the speaker himself* is the subject of the portrait, and being based on the (by no means imaginary) difficulty of demonstrating that fact to other people.

No. XXVII.—The Egg and the Cannon Ball. Solution.

You place the egg on the floor, in one corner of the room, in which position the walls on either side make it impossible to touch it with the cannon ball.

No. XXVIII.—A Curious Window. Solution.

The window was diamond-shaped. By enlarging it to a square its area is exactly doubled, without increasing either its height or width.

A window shaped as an isosceles or right-angled triangle will equally answer the conditions of the puzzle.

No. XXIX.—Queer Calculations. Solution.

Take the Roman equivalent for 101 (CI), and divide the two letters by inserting between them the equivalent for 50 (L). Add O, and you have CLIO, one of the nine Muses.

No. XXX.—An Arithmetical Enigma. Solution.

This is on the same principle. L stands for 50, the cipher for the letter O, and V for 5, while E is one-fifth of eight (e i g h t), the whole forming the word LOVE.

No. XXXI.—A Short Year. Solution.

It began on a Friday, and ended on Saturday.

No. XXXII.—The Mysterious Addition. Solution.

1. Write five in Roman characters (V); add I, and it becomes IV.
2. The letter S, which makes IX SIX.

No. XXXIII.—An Arithmetical Enigma. Solution.

Seven—Even—Eve.

No. XXXIV.—A New Valuation. Solution.

$8\frac{1}{4}$.

No. XXXV.—Easy, when You Know It. Solution.

Seven and one.

No. XXXVI.—Necessity the Mother of Invention. Solution.

Push the cork in.

No. XXXVII.—A Singular Subtraction. Solution.

$$
\begin{array}{ccc}
\text{SIX} & \text{IX} & \text{XL} \\
\text{IX} & \text{X} & \text{L} \\
\hline
\text{S} \quad \text{I} \quad \text{X}
\end{array}
$$

No. XXXVIII.—The Vanishing Number. Solution.

The number is 888. When halved it becomes $\frac{000}{000} = 0$.

No. XXXIX.—A Queer Query. Solution.

This is a mere " sell." The answer is " Letters." In the word " twenty " there are six letters, in the word "six" three, and so on.

No. XL.—The Mouse. Solution.

There were *nine* ears of corn in the box. The mouse brought out three *ears* at each journey, but two of them were his own.

No. XLI.—The Fasting Man. Solution.

One only; for after eating one his stomach would no longer be empty.

No. XLII.—The Family Party. Solution.

The very peculiar state of things described is accounted for as follows. The old gentleman was a widower, with a daughter and sister. The old gentleman and his father (who was also a widower) married two sisters (the wife of the old gentleman having a daughter by a former husband);

the old gentleman thus became his father's brother-in-law. The old gentleman's brother married the old gentleman's step-daughter; thus the old gentleman became his brother's father-in-law. The old gentleman's father-in-law married the old gentleman's sister, and the old gentleman thus became his father-in-law's brother-in-law. The old gentleman's brother-in-law married the old gentleman's daughter, whereby the old gentleman became his brother-in-law's father-in-law. He therefore himself filled all the four characters mentioned.

No. XLIII.—A Reversible Fraction. Solution.

$\frac{6}{9}$. Turn the paper upside down, so as to bring the denominator into the place of the numerator, and *vice versâ*. The fraction will still be $\frac{6}{9}$.

No. XLIV.—The Three Counters. Solution.

Remove one of the end counters and transfer it to the opposite end. You have not touched the middle counter, but it is no longer in the middle.

No. XLV.—Magic Made Easy.

This puzzle, like that last described, depends on a double meaning. The spectators naturally prepare themselves for some more or less adroit feat of jugglery, but you perform your undertaking by simply crossing the closed hands. The right hand (and the coin in it) is now where the left was previously, and *vice versâ*.